Preaching Paul

Preaching Paul

DANIEL PATTE

FORTRESS PRESS   PHILADELPHIA

Library of Congress Cataloging in Publication Data

Patte, Daniel.
  Preaching Paul.

  (Fortress resources for preaching)
  Includes index.
    1. Bible. N. T. Epistles of Paul—Homiletical use.
  I. Title. II. Series.
  BS2650.4.P37 1984   227′.06   84 – 47931
  ISBN 0 – 8006 – 1140 – 3 (pbk.)

K974B84   Printed in the United States of America   1 – 1140

to
Lewis Wilkins

Contents

Preface

This book is addressed primarily to preachers. This is obvious from the title "Preaching Paul," and from the fact that I engage in dialogue with preachers throughout the book. I am attempting to show what is involved in faithfully proclaiming Paul's Gospel as the "power of God for salvation" (Rom. 1:16). Yet this book is also addressed to a much larger audience, namely to all those who are called to witness to the power of the gospel and to offer themselves "as a living sacrifice" (Rom. 12:1). This is the vocation of the entire "body of Christ." Whether we fulfill this vocation from the pulpit or in our interactions with other people in our daily lives, our vocation is fundamentally the same. We are all called to be imitators of Paul, as he is of Christ (1 Cor. 11:1). Consequently, what I say here about preaching Paul can be directly applied by lay people as they strive faithfully to fulfill their own vocation. While they do not usually speak from the pulpit, they speak to other members of the church, at least in informal conversation. Thus, while they are not called to witness to the gospel in formal sermons, they are nevertheless called to witness to the gospel by and through their own "speeches." As we shall see, this does not entail making use of a religious or other-worldly language in our daily conversations. Witnessing to the power of God involves pointing out to our contemporaries where the power of God is manifested in their experience. Our vocation as preachers or lay people is *not* simply a matter of repeating Paul's teaching, rather it is a matter of expressing the gospel in terms of the experience of those to whom we speak. Thus, as they read this book, lay people should keep in mind their vocation, and that witnessing to the gospel is nothing but an informal way of preaching.

Here I am attempting to present as clearly and as concisely as possible the main features of Paul's teaching so as to focus the discussion upon its implications for preaching and witnessing to the gospel in contemporary situations. Therefore, I have kept the technical discussion of Paul's letters and footnotes to a minimum. If, however, readers are interested in a more complete discussion of particular texts or ideas, they should consult my systematic study of Paul's letters: *Paul's Faith and the Power of the Gospel: A Structural Introduction to the Pauline Letters* (Philadelphia: Fortress Press, 1983). While I explain each point by presenting an interpretation of central Pauline texts so that the present book may be understandable in and of itself, I do not undertake the critical discussion which establishes this interpretation over against other interpretations. Each reference to a text by Paul can be viewed as a footnote referring to the interpretation presented in *Paul's Faith and the Power of the Gospel* (see Indexes, 397 – 408). In that book one will also find suggestions for further reading at the end of my study of each letter.

A first draft of *Preaching Paul* was presented and discussed in the context of "Proclamation: An Intensive Preaching Clinic for the New Homiletic," organized by Cokesbury and co-sponsored by the Divinity School of Vanderbilt University in July of 1983. I wish to thank Ms. Debra Ball-Kilbourne for her excellent organization of the conference, and participants in this workshop for their probing questions and comments which helped me revise the first draft. I am also grateful to the members of the adult Sunday school class at Trinity Presbyterian Church, Nashville, Tenn. who graciously agreed to be a "testing ground" for the relevance of this book for lay people in the church. Pamela Thimmes, O.S.F., graduate student in New Testament, John A. Hollar of Fortress Press, and my colleague David G. Buttrick, patiently helped me revise the style of this book and clarify important points of its argument *grâce à leur esprit de finesse théologique*. Finally, I acknowledge with gratitude the support of the University Research Council of Vanderbilt University which, through a Summer Fellowship, assisted my new research project on Paul, the first fruit of which is this book.

Introduction

For Paul, preaching, in the broad sense of transmitting the gospel as "power of God for salvation," was an imperative, an urgent task that he pursued relentlessly. It was a demanding vocation which involved many risks. I refer not only to physical risks of persecution brought about by the boldness with which Paul confronted Gentiles and Jews with the gospel, but also to theological risks involved in expressing and embodying the gospel in such a way as to address Gentiles. As the church faithfully transmitted the gospel there were necessarily tensions between the church and the society in which it lived, and thus Paul warned believers that persecutions were to be expected (1 Thess. 3:4). His faithfulness also created tensions within the church, particularly among groups representing various tendencies. Often Paul deliberately provoked controversies (as in Gal. 2:11 – 21), rather than avoiding them by assuming a conciliatory attitude. We shall see that Paul's attitude was prompted not by arrogance, but by faithfulness to the demands of the gospel.

Preaching Paul, or being witnesses to the gospel in our lives, which involves "imitating" Paul (1 Cor. 11:1; see also 8:1—11:1), is consequently a perilous exercise. It demands that we take risks, even though we may long for security. It will exacerbate tensions within the church as well as between the church and our society, though we may wish for harmony in the church and for peaceful relations with the world. Yet it is through this "foolish" and scandalous proclamation alone that the gospel can be manifested as the power of God for salvation. The Reformers' preaching, Luther's in particular, offers a clear illustration of what happens when one undertakes the risk of preaching Paul: theological controversies, turmoil within the

11

church, disruption of relations between church and society, but also renewal of the church, and indeed of all parties involved.

As any generation, ours urgently needs to hear Paul's message. "And how are they to hear without a preacher?" (Rom. 10:14), that is, without a preacher who would accept a call to be sent, to proclaim the folly of the cross (1 Cor. 1:18 – 25), and to speak as a fool (2 Corinthians 11—12). We acquiesce. But all too often we end up betraying our vocation, though not intentionally. As Paul said of the Jews, we "have a zeal for God, but it is not enlightened" (Rom. 10:2), we have "ears that [do] not hear" (Rom. 11:8) Paul's message. Instead of taking the risk of transmitting the gospel as the power of God for salvation, we preach a riskless message about Paul's wisdom!

Our preaching of Paul is impaired by concerns which, in and of themselves, are commendable. It is enough here to consider two characteristic instances. One, we want to heed Paul's exhortation to "hold true to what we have attained" (Phil. 3:16) and cling to interpretations/preachings of Paul which have proved to be valuable for the Church over the ages. Two, we want to strive to present Paul's teaching faithfully by preaching exegetical sermons which explain in detail the meaning of his letters. In both cases, we often betray Paul's proclamation. In the first case, we deny the dynamic character of Paul's faith. In the second case, we confuse two types of discourses, exegesis and preaching, so that our "sermons" fail to achieve their proper goal.

The first and common temptation is to believe that we preach Paul when we repeat the Reformers' interpretation of Paul. Yet emphasis on Pauline concepts such as "justification through faith," "salvation by faith alone," or "predestination," was the result of an application of Paul's teaching to a specific situation, namely the sixteenth-century situation in which the Reformers had to confront specific corruptions of the gospel by the Roman Catholic Church of that time. It is good to remember earlier applications of Paul's teaching in order to avoid falling prey to the same corruptions of the gospel that the Reformers had to confront. This is "holding true to what we have attained" (Phil. 3:16). But, in the same text (Phil. 3:12 – 16), Paul emphasizes that we need to leave the past behind and look ahead, an essential characteristic of Paul's faith which needs to be accounted for in our preaching of Paul. In fact, the valid transmission of Paul's teaching involves applying it to our contemporary situation as the Reformers did to their own, and as Paul himself applied Christ's teaching to the new situation of a mission among the Gentiles. In Paul's case, his preaching of the gospel did not make any significant use of the central concept of Jesus' teaching—the Kingdom of God. Yet it is precisely because Paul did not simply repeat Jesus' teaching that he did in fact transmit the same faith. Transmitting the gospel as Paul understood, involves applying it constantly to new situations, and expressing it in terms of these new situations, rather than conveying a "pre-packaged" message. Consequently, *simply repeating* the Reformers' preaching of Paul is, in fact, betraying Paul's gospel. Ironically, today it is often in Catholic Church circles that one can find greater faithfulness to Paul's teaching, and thus to the Reformers' teaching! By these remarks I do not mean to say that concepts such as "justification through faith" are irrelevant for our preaching of Paul today. I merely want to emphasize that they need not be the focal point of our application of Paul's teaching to contemporary situations. In the present cultural, social, religious, and ecclesial setting, one might need to emphasize other aspects of Paul's teaching. I am also suggesting that preaching Paul cannot be limited to transmitting a knowledge of his theological views (cf. chap. 1).

A second temptation is to confuse preaching with other types of discourses prevalent in our culture. We have to acknowledge that preaching is different from lecturing and other kinds of public speech in that it is the communication of a religious message. Whether it is aimed at converting non-believers, or at nurturing the faith of believers, preaching is *the communication of a faith.* In order to achieve this end, sermons—the common medium of preachers—must have a form quite different from lectures and exegetical studies which aim at *communicating information about* the biblical texts and their teachings.

Preaching betrays its vocation and fails to achieve its goal when it merely *repeats* exegetical studies. Recent methodological studies in exegesis help us understand why. Today we witness a multiplication of exegetical methods: in addition to various kinds of historical-critical exegesis, there are sociological, literary, structural, hermeneutical, and materialistic exegesis.[1] Each of these methods provides access to biblical texts in terms of a specific modern view or conviction about what is truly meaningful in a text. Consequently, each of these exegetical studies is convincing only for those who share their specific view or conviction.

For example, a lecture presenting a historical exegesis is organized in such a way as to demonstrate convincingly to the hearers what is the historical meaning of a text: for example, how the text is related to the secular history of its time, or how a christological title is to be understood in view of Jewish and Hellenistic concepts which are part of the historical background of the New Testament. The lecture is a valid historical exegesis when it rigorously follows, and thus is organized according to, the demands, norms, and warrants of historiography. In other words, the exegetical discourse is organized according to convictions that historians share about what is truly meaningful.

What is the effect of such a historical lecture on hearers? It communicates *information about* a biblical text, but only to those who share the historians' convictions about what is truly meaningful. It may disclose some characteristics of the biblical faith expressed in these texts. But, interestingly enough, such a faith will be recognized as valid only by those who embrace "historical convictions." So the biblical faith is subordinated to the historians' faith (their convictions). The faith communicated or nurtured is the "historians' faith," that is, convictions about what is truly meaningful for historians, rather than the biblical faith. In addition, such a lecture communicates a certain *knowledge about* the biblical text, a knowledge of the biblical text from the point of view of the "historians' faith."

---

1. In the case of materialistic exegesis, see the 1974 French work of Fernando Belo, *A Materialist Reading of the Gospel of Mark*, Eng. trans. Matthew J. O'Connell (Maryknoll, N.Y.: Orbis Books, 1981); Michel Clevenot, *Approches materialistes de la Bible* (Paris: Editions du Cerf, 1976), Eng. trans. forthcoming from Orbis Books. See also work influenced by materialistic exegesis in *God of the Lowly: Socio-Historical Interpretations of the Bible*, ed. W. Schottroff and W. Stegemann (Eng. trans. Matthew J. O'Connell; Maryknoll, N.Y.: Orbis Books, 1984); and the report by Kuno Füssel, "The Materialist Reading of the Bible: Report on an Alternative Approach to Biblical Texts," in *The Bible and Liberation: Political and Social Hermeneutics*, ed. Norman K. Gottwald (Maryknoll, N.Y.: Orbis Books, 1983), 134 – 46.

One can readily understand what a disaster it is when a sermon is merely the repetition, often in a simplified way, of an exegetical study. The sermon fails to communicate the biblical faith *as faith* and, in fact, communicates the "historians' faith," or the "sociologists' faith" if it repeats a sociological exegesis, and so on and so forth!

Of course, as an exegete I do not intend to belittle exegesis. Exegesis has the essential role of elucidating characteristics of the faith expressed in the biblical texts. Furthermore, exegesis needs to use methodologies based upon modern views and convictions so that its description of the biblical faith may be understandable and meaningful for modern people, including preachers. Without critical exegesis preachers cannot *know* what characterizes the biblical faith which they are committed to proclaim. And then what would they proclaim? Thus, preachers must expose themselves to the results of exegesis. Yet a sermon is not an exegetical lecture. Indeed, just as a lecture does, so a sermon needs to communicate a knowledge of the biblical texts, that is, information about the biblical texts. But, unlike a lecture, a sermon's primary function is to *communicate the biblical faith as faith that hearers can make their own.* Consequently, a sermon should not merely be a talk about biblical faith. It needs to embody biblical faith. It needs to be a discourse which is organized according to the demands of the biblical faith that it aims to transmit, not according to the demands of "another faith," such as the convictions about what is truly meaningful to historians, sociologists, literary critics, structuralists, or materialistic exegetes.

Preaching involves, therefore, transmitting the faith expressed in the biblical texts in such a way that our hearers can share it. This means that the exegetical preparation of our sermons needs to be primarily concerned with elucidating the characteristics of the faith expressed in these texts. Most types of biblical exegesis contribute in one way or another to this elucidation, yet some of them do so more directly than others. Such is the case of structural exegesis which allows the exegete to focus directly upon important characteristics of an author's faith.

This book is based upon the results of structural exegesis of Paul's letters. It owes several of its strategies to the structural approach.

First, the distinction between *lectures* and *sermons*, as well as the correlative distinction between "theological ideas" and "faith as system of convictions," is based upon semiotic and structural research. This research is devoted to the study of the phenomenon of communication and allows us to discern a plurality of dimensions of meaning, such as theological ideas and convictions, and their interrelations. These issues are presented in non-technical terms in Chapters 1 and 6 of *Paul's Faith and the Power of the Gospel.*

Second, structural exegesis describes how Paul's faith functions, that is, how it leads him to interrelate all the elements of his experience according to a certain pattern. This faith pattern can be found in the way in which Paul perceives the relationship between God and human beings. Yet, it is also expressed more concretely in the way in which Paul perceives the relationship between Christ and the Jews, between Paul and his churches, and so forth. Structural exegesis and its results can thus help preachers identify the characteristics of the faith presented in Paul's letters—the exegetical preparation of the sermon. Then the preachers are in a position to organize their sermons so that they may truly embody that faith. Such sermons will indeed communicate that faith, and not merely a knowledge of that faith.

My structural exegesis of Paul's letters led me to conclude that Paul's faith is most fundamentally characterized by three interrelated features. It is *charismatic*, *typological*, and *eschatological*.[2]

In brief, one can say that the faith which Paul aims to transmit through his letters is *charismatic* in the sense that it involves the conviction that the believers can directly discover, through faith, revelatory manifestations of God in their experience. Paul perceives the message about Christ (the *kerygma*) as the type and the promise of God's manifestations in the believers' experience, as the Old Testament was a type and a promise of God's manifestation in Christ, and is also a type of God's manifestations in the believers' experience. This is why Paul's faith can be called *typological*. In spite of this experience no believer can claim to have the complete and final

2. Daniel Patte, *Paul's Faith and the Power of the Gospel: A Structural Introduction to the Pauline Letters* (Philadelphia: Fortress Press, 1983), 233 – 41. Hereafter, *PFPG.*

revelation: we shall see "face to face" and "understand fully" (1 Cor. 13:12) only in the eschatological time—the time of the judgment, when Christ will return, the Parousia (e.g., 1 Thess. 4:13—5:11; 1 Cor. 15:20 – 28). The manifestations and revelations of God that believers discover in their own experiences are themselves promises of the eschatological manifestation and revelation. Consequently, Paul's faith can be called *eschatological*. These charismatic, typological, and eschatological convictions are not only the basis of the faith and hope of the believers, but also, as we shall see, what allows the believers to love.

Reflecting on these and other results of my exegesis of Paul's letters, I will proceed by laying down a series of *Theses* concerning the characteristic features of Paul's faith for proclamation. Without repeating the entire exegesis, I then discuss in a series of commentarylike *Notes* the passages of Paul's letters which enabled me to formulate each of the theses.

In order to learn how to preach Paul's gospel, there is no better teacher than Paul himself. We can thus begin our study by considering passages in which he speaks about preaching (Romans 10, in particular). Yet we should not limit ourselves to these passages. We also need to discern in Paul's letters how he himself goes about the task of transmitting and nurturing the Christian faith. In so doing we will discover that for Paul the transmission of the gospel is not merely the proclamation of a message—the message about Christ's death and resurrection. This transmission also involves helping others to recognize manifestations of God, or Christ, in their experiences, and to understand how they should respond to these manifestations of the divine. Since the gospel is for Paul the "power of God for salvation" (Rom. 1:16), its transmission has to come through prophetic preaching, that is, a preaching which points out where and how this power is manifested in the experience of the believers.

This characteristic of Paul's teaching is often not perceived because our contemporary view of religious experience is quite different from his. For some of us, a religious experience is primarily a private, subjective, individual matter. Clearly this is the case in

evangelical circles where individual conversion and spiritual experience, as well as personal and direct relationship with God and
Christ are emphasized. But this is also the case in more liberal circles, *in spite of* many disclaimers. It is not by chance that popular
studies of "faith development" focus upon the dynamics by which
individuals grow and mature in faith. From such a perspective we
do not recognize that Paul constantly speaks of God's manifestations *in the experience of believers* to whom he writes, because in
many instances he points to situations beyond the private and individual spiritual experience of his readers.

Nevertheless, Paul's view of the religious experience as broader
than an individual experience is not foreign to us, as Lewis Wilkins
discovered in an experiment that he repeated in various contexts. It
is a matter of asking the right question so as to overcome the pre-
understanding of the participants that spiritual experience is purely
individual. Wilkins asked the following questions: "What are the
social dynamics in the life of a congregation . . . that help or hinder
the development of mature Christians, that 'grow' folk in faith and
knowledge?" It is worth quoting a few paragraphs from Wilkins:

> When people talk about times in their lives when they "grew in
> faith and knowledge," they rarely tell stories about formal, structured
> learning situations. If they talk about an experience in Sunday school,
> college or seminary, it almost never has anything to do with the *con-
> tent* of the curriculum that was being taught.
> What people do talk about in those growth stories are times in their
> lives when they were somehow *in transition*.
> They talk about events that occurred when they were moving from
> being single to being married—or from being married to being single.
> They talk about what happened to them in moving from being chil-
> dren to being parents, after the birth of their first child. They talk
> about transitions brought about by the death of a parent or spouse.
> They talk about what happened to them between pulling up roots in
> one place and putting down roots in a new place far away. They talk
> about events that occurred between graduation from high school and
> becoming secure in the role of wage-earner or student. They describe
> what happened between getting fired from one job and getting hired
> in another one. . . .
> Many or even most of the experiences of growth that I have heard
> people describe are the result of unplanned, disruptive interventions
> into their lives from outside, interventions over which they have no

control. Even those that are somehow anticipated—the death of a spouse, the long-predicted loss of a job, a divorce ending a marriage that long had been an empty shell—have about them when they actually occur an inescapable dimension of the uncontrollable and unpredictable. I tend to think that this dimension is an essential, not merely accidental part of what makes for growth in faith and knowledge.[3]

Wilkins concludes that these experiences have to be viewed as manifestations of "divine powers" and quotes these lines from Julian Hartt:

We ought to say that [a person] is not really religious unless he feels that some power is bearing down on him, unless, that is, he believes he must do something about divine powers who have done something about him.[4]

This quotation echoes Paul who, by transmitting the gospel, aimed at helping people discover the "power of God for salvation." God's power is bearing down on them in uncontrollable and unpredictable ways, in the most unexpected places of their lives—not merely in their private spiritual life—and in the most unlikely situations. If the manifestation of the power of God is indeed what is, for Paul, central to the transmission of the gospel, our preaching of the gospel cannot but be prophetic; it needs to include the proclamation of God's manifestations in the present of our hearers. In preparation for preaching, it then becomes essential for us to learn from Paul how to discern just what are and what are not manifestations of God.

3. Lewis Wilkins, unpublished paper, "Eucharist and Growth: Theological Reflection on Strategies for Nurture."

4. Julian N. Hartt, *A Christian Critique of American Culture: An Essay in Practical Theology* (New York: Harper & Row, 1967). James M. Gustafson quotes these lines from Hartt as an expression of what is central to his view of religion, namely "affectivity" as "evoked by a power or powers that limit and sustain life in the world." See Gustafson's *Ethics from a Theocentric Perspective: Theology and Ethics* (Chicago: University of Chicago Press, 1981), 1:196 – 97.

1
Proclamation of the Word and Transmission of the Gospel

In a first series of theses, and through the examination of central texts, we aim to characterize how we should preach Paul.

THESIS 1

The proclamation of the Word (kerygma) is *necessary*, indeed *essential* (Romans 10), for the transmission of the gospel, that is, for the transmission and the nurture of the Christian faith, but it is *not sufficient*.

Notes

1. As we read the text beginning in Rom. 10:14, we should note that the argument does not stop with 10:17, "So faith comes from what is heard, and what is heard comes by the preaching of Christ." This verse needs to be set in its full context: Rom. 10:14—11:10. It then appears that "preaching Christ" is *necessary* for faith, since "faith comes from what is heard." It is clearly *not sufficient*, however, since Israel has heard (10:18) and yet has failed to believe, as is expressed in 11:7 – 12 and in 9:1—10:4.

What was the problem? "Did Israel not understand?" (10:19). In fact they did. They were made "angry" by Moses. They were "a disobedient" and "contrary people." How could they be "disobedient" and "contrary" if they did not understand? They have heard and understood the message, but they have rejected it. Why? Because they have "a spirit of stupor," "eyes that [do] not see, ears that [do] not hear." (Paul quotes from Deut. 29:3 or, more likely, from Isa. 29:10 and Isa. 6:9 – 10). They have "darkened eyes"

(Rom. 11:8 – 10; quotation from Ps. 67 [68]:23 – 24). As parallel
passages in Romans (1:18 – 32; 7:13 – 25) show, this means that
Israel did hear the message—the Jews did understand that it was
the Word of God—but they failed to apply it properly. They were
disobedient, because, in another sense of the term, they failed to
"understand" it, they have a "spirit of stupor" and "eyes which [do]
not see," "darkened eyes."

From our brief examination of Rom. 10:14—11:10, we can conclude that two conditions need to be met so that the Christian faith
may be transmitted to non-believers. On the one hand, Christ needs
to be preached to these people. On the other hand, they need to be
delivered from their "spirit of stupor."

2. Another text will help us progress: 1 Cor. 13:8 – 13. Note that
Paul contrasts "faith, hope, and love" with "knowledge, prophecy
and tongues." Faith is not to be confused with "knowing something,"
including knowing the great sacred mysteries—from prophets or
ecstatic/spiritual experiences. Yet, as the Corinthians, we often
think, or act as if we think, that transmitting knowledge—
preaching a message, proclaiming the Word—is transmitting or
nurturing faith. For us, when people "know" the right things (for
example, the message of the gospel, the correct theology) and
accept them as true (that is, as coming from God), they have faith.
But obviously, such a view contradicts Paul's text.

We confuse the proclamation of a message or Word—preaching
as teaching—with the transmission of the Christian faith, that is,
the transmission of the gospel as the "power of God for salvation."

Is this a valid interpretation of 1 Cor. 13:8 – 13? Is not Paul constantly speaking about "preaching the gospel?" Does he not think of
his ministry primarily as "preaching the gospel?" An examination of
the texts show that such is NOT the case, although, as we have seen,
preaching/transmitting the message or Word is certainly a significant part of his ministry.[5] Confusion results, in part, from translat-

---

5. The image of Paul as constantly preaching to crowds has its origin in Acts. From
his sociological perspective, Wayne Meeks (*The First Urban Christians: The Social
World of the Apostle Paul* [New Haven, Conn.: Yale University Press, 1983], 25 – 32)
implies conclusions similar to ours. Paul's involvement in the daily life of urban people was an essential part of his transmission of the gospel.

ing two different Greek verbs—*kerysso* and *euaggelizo*—by a single English verb, "to preach." While the first, *kerysso*, does mean "to preach," as in Romans 10, the latter, *euaggelizo*, which is usually translated "to preach the gospel," has in fact a broader meaning, which can be seen when one examines the contexts in which this verb is used. It is better to translate *euaggelizo* literally by "to evangelize," or by "to transmit the gospel."[6]

Thus we can conclude that preaching or teaching a message is *necessary and essential* to the transmission of the gospel as the "power of salvation," but is *not sufficient*.

THESIS 2

The proclamation of the Word is *not sufficient* for the transmission of the gospel because the gospel is for Paul "the power of God for salvation" (Rom. 1:16). The gospel involves manifestations of the power of God. Without manifestations of God, the message or Word is powerless.

Notes

1. On the surface, there is nothing new in this thesis. Surely, it is clear to everybody that without God's manifestation our preaching of the message is powerless. Yet the question arises: what is the nature of this manifestation of God which makes the gospel "the power of God for salvation"? There are several possible answers:

6. The passages where Paul uses *euaggelizo* can be easily identified in the translations of Paul's letters. Each time we read in them the phrase "preach the gospel" or "proclaim the gospel," this is a translation of *euaggelizo*, and thus should be read "transmit the gospel." There are only two exceptions, Gal. 2:2 and 1 Thess. 2:9, where Paul speaks of "preaching the gospel" using *kerysso*, in the contexts of discussions regarding the content of the message he preaches. Similarly, when Paul uses the term *kerygma* (Rom. 16:25; 1 Cor. 1:21; 2:4; 15:14), it refers to the content of the "message" which is "folly" as long as it is taken independently from the accompanying manifestations of God. See Joseph A. Fitzmyer, S.J., "The Gospel in the Theology of Paul," in *Interpreting the Gospels*, ed. James L. Mays (Philadelphia: Fortress Press, 1981), 1 – 13. In this essay, Fitzmyer correctly notes that the transmission of the gospel involves the proclamation of the lordship of Christ. Yet he fails to recognize that it means that the proclamation of the *kerygma* about Jesus' death and resurrection is the proclamation of a promise (p. 10), the promise that Christ as Lord does intervene as manifestations of the power of God in the present of the believers. Thus while Fitzmyer recognizes the "promissory nature" of the gospel, he interprets it merely as fulfillment of Old Testament promises. See below Thesis 3.

a. *The manifestation of God in Jesus, and especially in his death and resurrection.* In light of Romans 9—11, this is clearly not the case. God's manifestation in Christ's death and resurrection failed to be, for most of the Jews, "the power of God for salvation." The manifestation of God in the death and resurrection of Christ is essential: without it there is no gospel. It was an effective intervention of God, but for Paul, it is not sufficient.

b. *The manifestation of God in the process of preaching the message.* Obviously, this is also necessary: preaching can be, and needs to be, related to the gifts of the Spirit (1 Cor. 12:4 – 11); preaching needs to be tested by God (1 Thess. 2:4). Without the manifestation of God, no one would be called and sent (Rom. 10:15); there would be no valid preaching. The text of Romans 10 presupposes that preachers have been sent by God, and that their preaching is valid. Yet this preaching is powerless. Beyond the necessary intervention of God in the proclamation of God's manifestation in Christ, another manifestation of God is still needed.

c. *The manifestation of God in the experience of the hearers.* It is this third kind of manifestation of God which transforms the message *about* Christ and *about* God's manifestation in Christ into the gospel as the power of God for salvation.

2. As we acknowledge the necessity of the manifestation of God in the experience of the hearers to transform our message into the gospel as the power of God for salvation, we might think we have nothing to do about this aspect of the transmission of the gospel, except "to pray that God intervene in the experience of our hearers." Of course we need to pray in this way. Yet, *in our preaching and in our ministry we also have to assume responsibility for this manifestation of God in our hearers' experience.*

My statement may seem outrageous and even blasphemous. Obviously, I do not mean that we can make God intervene, or that we should try to intervene in God's place! Furthermore, if God's manifestation in the experience of the hearers is merely God's transformation of our message (human words) into the divine Word (a Word of power) by altering the mind of our hearers, then there is nothing we can do and need to do, besides pray. But God's manifestation in the hearers' experience is much more than this, just as the gospel promises.

THESIS 3

The Proclamation of the message of the Gospel is *the proclamation of a promise*. It is the proclamation that through Christ God has reconciled the world to himself. The reconciliation is the promise that, after Christ, God does intervene in human affairs, and consequently in the experience of our hearers, instead of abandoning us to the "custody of the Law as pedagogue."

Notes

1. As we read Gal. 3:6 – 9, note that what Abraham received was a promise: "In you shall all the nations be blessed." Note also that Paul introduces this quotation by the phrase "God . . . preached the Gospel beforehand (*proeuēggelisato*) to Abraham."

For Paul, gospel is promise and thus the promise to Abraham is gospel. We find the same assertion in Gal. 3:22: "But the scripture consigned all things to sin, that what was promised to faith in Jesus Christ might be given to those who believe." This verse can refer both to the promises of Scripture (promises to Abraham, Gal. 3:16, 21), or, as in the Revised Standard Version, to the promise which the gospel of Jesus Christ is all about.

That the gospel is promise can also be seen throughout the letters by comparing how Paul uses the Old Testament and the *kerygma*. Such a study shows that Paul uses both of them as types, that is, prophecies, prefigurations, thus promises of later manifestations of God.[7]

2. In Gal. 3:6 – 29 Paul refers to three periods:

a. *The period before the Law*, that is, the period of Abraham when promises were given *and* fulfilled (Romans 4), and when faith was possible.

b. *The period of the Law* (Gal. 3:17) when faith was not possible

---

7. See Patte, *PFPG*, Chaps. 4 and 6.

("before faith came," 3:23) and, we can infer, when the promises
were not fulfilled.

   c. *The period which began with Christ* when faith was again
possible ("until Christ came" Gal. 3:24, "now that faith has come"
3:25) and when promises were fulfilled (3:22).

The proclamation of the gospel is a proclamation which affirms
that since the time of Christ we are in a new period of sacred history,
a period in which God fulfills his promises, including the promises
contained in Jesus Christ. In other words, we live in the eschatological time where God already fulfills his promises, even though they
will be completely fulfilled only at the time of the Parousia (when
"we shall see face to face," according to 1 Cor. 13:12).

   3. The question arises, why should God fulfill his promises in the
time after Christ since humankind is as sinful now as it was during
the period of the Law? For Paul, the answer is simple: because of
Jesus' death on the cross. This is what he expresses in 2 Cor.
5:17 – 21: "In Christ God was reconciling the world to himself, not
counting their trespasses against them" (v. 19). Similarly, in Rom.
5:6 – 21 Paul designates what is achieved in Christ by both "reconciliation" and "justification." Clearly the work of Christ should not
be confused with "justification through faith," since this reconcilia-
tion/justification is for "the world" (Rom. 5:18), the whole of
humankind, and not merely for the believers. Note also that we
were justified/reconciled "while we were enemies" (Rom. 5:10).

   4. Our proclamation of the gospel therefore needs to be the proclamation of the "reconciliation" (2 Cor. 5:18 – 20), which includes
the proclamation that we are in the period in which God fulfills his
promises, that is, the period in which God intervenes again in
human affairs. God's promise is not only for the believers but for
everyone.

Our proclamation of the gospel is also the proclamation of the
possibility of faith. But then, what is faith for Paul? We can now
understand that faith is more than merely knowing and acknowledging as valid the message that God intervened in Christ. Faith
also involves viewing the cross as reconciliation of the world to God,
and thus as promise that God will intervene in human affairs in our
time. Faith is trusting that God intervened in Christ, but it is also

taking hold of God's promise and looking for, and indeed seeing, God at work in our experience, and, of course, acting accordingly.

THESIS 4

The proclamation of the gospel as the "power of God for salvation" involves both the proclamation of the Word/message/promise AND the proclamation of how and when God intervenes in the hearers' experience. When preaching does not proclaim such fulfillment of the promise of the gospel, it is unwittingly conveying a belief in justification through works instead of a belief in justification through faith.

Notes

1. It is, of course, much safer to limit our preaching to a repetition and an explanation of the message/promise of the gospel, that is, transmitting a "knowledge" of the gospel, *without* proclaiming how and when God's promise is fulfilled in our present. But in so doing we are denying the promise. We are showing that we do not have faith—faith which "sees" that indeed God fulfills his promises and more specifically, the promise included in reconciliation. Actually, we have transformed the gospel into a "dead letter"—just as the Jews, according to Paul, had transformed their Scripture into a dead and deadly letter (2 Cor. 3:6 – 7). This is a serious matter. Whatever we may say about the "power of the gospel" in our preaching, if we fail to point to fulfillments of the promises of the gospel, we convey to our hearers that the gospel is in fact powerless and thus that we cannot count on God's manifestation in our experience. Then, since we are not established in relationship with God by discovering through faith God's manifestation in our experience ("justification through faith"), we are condemned to seek to establish ourselves in relation with God through our own good works ("justification through works" of the Law or "through works" of the gospel!).

When we examine our preaching, we have to acknowledge that against our own wishes we often convey a belief in "justification through works." We do so each time we exhort our hearers to live a good Christian life, a spiritual life, a life of service, to be a loving community, *without grounding our exhortations in the fulfillments* of the promise of the gospel in their experience.

2. Preaching the gospel as the power of God for salvation is a prophetic task. We are understandably uneasy with prophetic preaching. Much of the "witnessing" to God's and Jesus' manifestations we hear around us seems overly "enthusiastic"—precisely the same "enthusiasm" and "spirituality" which Paul was fighting in Corinth (1 Cor. 4:8 – 13; 2 Corinthians 10—12)! Similarly, much of contemporary "prophetic preaching"—declarations of the fulfillment of scriptural prophecies in the political events of our time that we often hear on radio or TV—sounds like a message comparable to that of the Jewish apocalyptists (for example, the Zealots) rather than to the gospel.

From the very beginning of his ministry Paul had to fight and resist these distortions of the gospel. In his first letter, for instance, Paul exhorts his readers to "test everything," while warning them "not to quench the Spirit" and "not to despise prophecy" (1 Thess. 5:19 – 21). The presence of false prophetic preaching and witnessing does not deny the need for true prophetic preaching of the gospel as the power of God for salvation.

3. Such prophetic preaching is necessarily a "gift of the Spirit" (1 Cor. 12:4 – 11). This means, among other things, that such preaching is to be prepared in prayer. But, what kind of prayer? What is prayer for Paul? Prayer does involve intercessions, that is, asking for God's intervention in one's experience (see 2 Cor. 12:8), or in other people's experience. For instance, Paul prays for the Romans (Rom. 1:9 – 10) and asks them to pray for him (15:30 – 32). For Paul, though, intercession is always associated with *thanksgiving:* "Rejoice always, pray constantly, give thanks in all circumstances; for this is the will of God in Christ Jesus for you" (1 Thess. 5:16 – 18). Each of Paul's letters, except Galatians, begins with a thanksgiving prayer such as "we give thanks to God always for you all, constantly mentioning you in our prayers" (1 Thess. 1:2). We must conclude that thanksgiving is a primary component of prayer for Paul.

We also need to ask, thanksgiving about what? In other parts of the New Testament (including the Deutero-Pauline letters such as

Ephesians) thanksgivings are often related to God's manifestation in Jesus Christ and to the work of Christ on the cross. Not so in Paul's letters. His thanksgivings are primarily focused upon God's manifestations in the experience of his hearers and in his own experience. In other words, Paul gives thanks for God's *present* manifestations, rather than for God's manifestations in the past. There is, of course, nothing wrong with thanking God for what he did in the past. But, according to Paul, prayer necessarily includes giving thanks for God's manifestations *in the present*.

In preparation for preaching we need, therefore, to "pray constantly and give thanks in all circumstances" (1 Thess. 5:17 – 18). Such prayer involves *contemplation*, the contemplation of what is happening in our present world and in the experience of the people with whom we interact so that we may discover God's manifestations. How can we give thanks for what God is doing in our present if we do not discover it? And how can we discover God's manifestations without the assistance of the Spirit? Only through faith—a gift of the Spirit (1 Cor. 12:9)—can we hope to discern the manifestations of God in our present. Yet we need more than the assistance of the Spirit to guide us in our prayer of thanksgiving. As is clear in the case of the Corinthians who were very "spiritual," we also need to "distinguish between spirits" (1 Cor. 12:10) and to "test everything" (1 Thess. 5:21).

The transmission of the gospel as the power of God for salvation, therefore, needs to include the proclamation of how and where God intervenes in our hearers' experience. But how can we do so without first discovering these manifestations ourselves and giving thanks for them? And how can we ward off false prophecy without testing everything? In other words, the transmission of the gospel as the power of God for salvation demands careful preparation.

Paul's letters are an excellent guide for preparing ourselves to proclaim the gospel. This is not by chance. Among other things, the letters exhort readers to carry out their vocation as faithful witnesses of the gospel. Paul achieves this, in part, by showing his readers how he discovers the fulfillment of the gospel as promise in their common experience, and by disclosing how he tests the validity of this discovery. Yet in Paul's letters we do not find specific passages which could be viewed as a treatise on "the spiritual exercises needed for discovering and testing the fulfillment of the gospel"! Rather, "method" and "criteria" are an intrinsic part of the faith that Paul aims at transmitting. They are, therefore, embodied in the very argument of his letters. In short, Paul's letters are given as models of the way in which one looks at one's experience through faith and discovers in it the fulfillment of the gospel. Consequently, preparing ourselves to transmit the gospel as the power of God for salvation involves a close reading of Paul's letters aimed at discerning how Paul implements his faith. In Chapter 2 we will sketch the main results of such an investigation, which is necessary so that, in turn, our proclamation may embody the faith in the gospel as promise of God's manifestations in our present experience.

If Paul discloses to *his readers* how to discover in their experience the fulfillment of the gospel, then our preaching should not only be the proclamation of the gospel in our hearers' experience but also an invitation for them to discover the manifestations of God in their present. This is what Paul's letters do and what our preaching should do. In this way our preaching will not merely be the proclamation of a word, the transmission of a knowledge about what God did for us in Jesus Christ, *as if* this were the last significant manifestation of God, and *as if* we could be saved by the mere knowledge of this word. Furthermore, our preaching will not be the unintentional transmission of a belief in justification through works. Rather, it will be the transmission of the gospel as the "power of God for salvation." Thanks to our preaching, our hearers will be in a position to discover the power of God at work in their experience. As in the case of Paul's transmission of the gospel so also our preaching will transmit it "not only in word but also in power and in the Holy Spirit and with full conviction" (1 Thess.1:5).

2
Discovering the
Fulfillments of the Gospel

In light of our examination of important passages of Paul's letters, it is clear that preaching Paul involves (1) proclaiming the gospel as a promise, (2) proclaiming the fulfillment of the gospel in our hearers' experience, and (3) inviting our hearers to discover for themselves this fulfillment.

Clearly, such preaching demands special attention to the exegesis of Paul's letters in *preparation for our preaching*. We need to learn from Paul how to discover in our present the fulfillment of the gospel as promise. To do so, we need to perform an exegesis of Paul's letters which will address specific questions to the texts: What are the types of situations in which Paul discovered God at work in his readers' experience and in his own? How did he discover these manifestations of God and establish that they were indeed true manifestations of God or of Christ? What did he view as incorrect identifications of the fulfillment of the gospel?

I will now present only the most important results of such an exegesis so as to suggest general guidelines for our preaching of Paul. In other words, this chapter should not be construed as taking the place of the exegesis that we, as preachers, need to perform in preparing each sermon. Even the detailed study of each letter does not take the place of the preacher's own exegesis.[8] Indeed, we constantly need to learn anew how to recognize God's or Christ's manifestations in our present.

One might wonder, do we really need to engage constantly in this

8. See Patte, *PFPG*, the guidebook for such an exegesis.

kind of exegesis? Do we not know how to recognize God's manifestations? Paul's answer would be a resounding "No." What we identify as "from God" is not necessarily from God, and what we
identify as evil, blasphemous or against God, might in fact be from
God. As we often confess, we are sinners—which means, according
to Paul, that we are under the power of sin. Thus we are "futile in
[our] thinking and [our] senseless minds [are] darkened" (Rom.
1:21). We have "eyes that [do] not see and ears that [do] not hear"
(Rom. 11:8). We know what is right and we want to do it, but we
find ourselves doing the evil we do not want to do (Rom. 7:14, 23;
1:32). Thus, even though we might see God's manifestations, we do
not necessarily recognize them for what they are. Yet this hopeless
situation is finally not hopeless: "Thanks be to God through Jesus
Christ our Lord!" (Rom. 7:25). The gospel as the power for salvation is also for us and our preaching! In order to benefit from the
power of the gospel we first need to "hear the message of the Gospel" (Thesis 5). Then we need to allow Paul to guide us to where we
should look so that our eyes may truly see (Thesis 6). We need to
understand the types of situations in which Paul saw God at work
(Theses 7 and 8). Then we will be in a position to be "imitators" of
Paul for our hearers, as he was an "imitator" of Christ for his readers
(Theses 9 and 10).

THESIS 5

For Paul, the message about Christ is threefold. It involves the repetition of the story of Christ's death and resurrection, the announce-
ment of his role at the Parousia, and the affirmation that already in
the present he is the Lord. But the core of the message is the story of
Christ's death and resurrection.

Notes

1. This message about Christ is summarized by Paul in several
well-known passages: 1 Cor. 15:3 – 8, Phil. 2:6 – 11, 1 Thess. 1:10.
As these passages and the rest of Paul's letters show, the core of the
message about Christ is the story of his death and resurrection.
Christ's death is God's reconciliation of the world to himself.

Christ's death re-opens the possibility of God's intervention in the present life of the believers as well as at the Parousia when the Lord will deliver us from the wrath to come (1 Thess. 1:10), participate in the judgment (Rom. 2:16), and deliver the kingdom to God (1 Cor. 15:24). Similarly, Christ's resurrection is not merely a matter of being raised from the dead but also of being *raised to the right hand of God* and receiving Lordship (Phil. 2:9 – 11). The resurrection means that Jesus is now Lord, "destroying every rule and every authority and power. For he must reign until he has put all his enemies under his feet" (1 Cor. 15:24 – 25). Thus the present activity of Jesus as Lord and his future activity at the Parousia are the direct consequences of his death and resurrection, the core of the message.

2. The interventions of the Lord in the present experience of the believers are, on the one hand, the fulfillment of the cross and resurrection and, on the other hand, prefigurations or preliminary manifestations of the interventions of the Lord at the Parousia. It is this overall message of the gospel that we need to hear if we want to identify the actual manifestations of the Lord in our present.

THESIS 6

Paul sees God at work in situations which are Christ-like, that is, in situations which include both a cross-like experience and a resurrection-like experience.

Notes

1. In 1 Thessalonians, following a thanksgiving for God's manifestation in his readers' experience, Paul explains what convinced him that God is really at work among them. He knows that they are "beloved by God" and "chosen" by God because of what happened when he was among them; when he preached the gospel to them there were miracles and manifestations of the Spirit. "For our gospel came to you not only in word, but also in power [miracle] and in the Holy Spirit and with full conviction" (1 Thess. 1:5). Yet he also thanks God, believing that God is somehow responsible, for their "work of faith and labor of love and steadfastness of hope in our Lord Jesus Christ" (1 Thess. 1:3). He explains the reasons for his

thanksgiving: "And you became imitators of us and of the Lord, for you received the word in much affliction, with joy inspired by the Holy Spirit; so that you became an example [Greek, *typos* or literally, "type"] to all the believers in Macedonia and in Achaia" (1 Thess. 1:6 – 7). Paul again uses the technical term "imitator" in 1 Thess. 2:14 – 15: "For you became imitators of the churches of God in Christ Jesus which are in Judea; for you suffered the same things from your own countrymen as they did from the Jews, who killed both the Lord Jesus and the prophets, and drove us out."

The term "imitator" clearly does not refer to a person following the example of another.[9] The Thessalonians are "imitators" of Paul, of the churches of Judea, of the Lord Jesus, primarily because the same things, or more precisely, similar things, *happened* to them. Being persecuted is not something that one does to oneself! On the positive side, in spite of persecutions, they are joyous. But, for Paul, this joy is not their doing. It is a "joy inspired by the Holy Spirit" (1 Thess. 1:6).

Thus Paul recognizes God's manifestation in the Thessalonians' experience because it is *"Christ-like."*

a. As Christ submitted himself to the will of God, they "received the word" and, therefore, submitted themselves to the will of God. In such a case we can say that being imitators means following the example of Christ—the meaning of the term imitator to which we are accustomed.

b. As Christ died on the cross, they suffered persecution. As such their experience is "cross-like." Being imitators is not doing something, but being objects of persecution caused by their fellow citizens, as Christ was crucified by the Jews (1 Thess. 2:15).

c. As Christ was raised from the dead by God, they have a "joy inspired by the Holy Spirit." As such their experience is resurrection-like. Here again, being imitators is not doing something. As God intervened and raised Jesus from the dead, through his Spirit, God intervened in the experience of the persecuted Thessalonians by giving them joy.

By being "imitators" of Christ the Thessalonians are also imita-

9. For further explanation, see Patte, *PFPG*, 131 – 39.

tors of Paul (and of the churches of Judea) since he is himself an "imitator" of Christ. Consequently Paul can say elsewhere: "Be imitators of me, as I am of Christ" (1 Cor. 11:1). But the criterion by which one discovers manifestations of God in present experience remains the same. True manifestations of God are to be found in "Christ-like" situations. The promise of the gospel of reconciliation is that God intervenes in our experience *as he did in Christ's experience*. In other words, God's manifestations in our present are of a similar "type" to God's manifestation in Jesus. Jesus is a "type" for believers. So also Paul as a Christ-like one is "type" for the Thessalonians. In turn, the Thessalonians, insofar as they are Christ-like, are type for the next generation of believers, that is, the Macedonians and the Achaians (1 Thess. 1:7).

2. My study of the other letters of Paul, focusing on what Paul views as manifestations of God in his experience and in his readers' experience, shows that the preceding observations hold true in every case, even though Paul may use different vocabulary to express the relations between the believers' experience and Christ's death and resurrection.[10] In fact, the phrase "in Christ" designates people who are Christ-like, that is, people to whom something like that which happened to Christ also happened.

3. That the "Christ-like" principle was an important, indeed an essential, part of Paul's gospel can be seen in 1 and 2 Corinthians. The controversies that Paul had with the Corinthian church concerned in large part the incorrect understanding that the Corinthians had of the cross. It is not that they did not believe that "Christ died for our sins" on the cross. Paul does not need to argue this point. The issue is rather that the Corinthians would not believe that they should suffer and be subjugated by evil powers as Christ was (1 Cor. 2:8).

The case of the Corinthians is most important for our purpose because it concerns the identification of God's manifestations in the present of believers. The situation can be summarized as follows: The Corinthians believed that the gospel was the promise that God would intervene in present experience. But, according to Paul, their

10. See Patte, *PFPG*, Chaps. 4—6.

identification of God's manifestations was totally confused and wrong. For them, the death of Christ for their sins meant that true believers, those who put themselves to the benefit of his death, were forever freed from any form of suffering. For them all the good things, including spiritual gifts, which happened to a believer were manifestations of God. By contrast, anybody who suffered in one way or another could not be a true believer. Since Paul was persecuted, poor, and sick, he could not be a true believer. Consequently he was not a true apostle.

Paul responds to them quite strongly, not primarily because he is personally rejected by the Corinthians, but because the whole gospel is at stake. The message about Christ, which is the "type" of the manifestations of God in our experience, is the proclamation (*kerygma*) of both the death *and* the resurrection of Christ, and not merely his resurrection. For the Corinthians, any resurrection-like experience, any good thing which happened to someone, was a manifestation of God (see Paul's sarcastic comments in 1 Cor. 4:8 – 13). For Paul, it is not so, even when these "good things" are spiritual gifts. Beside the Spirit of God there are evil spirits, and thus one must distinguish the spirits. One needs to use a full range of criteria to identify true manifestations of God. God can be said to have intervened in a Christ-like manner only in a situation which is *both* cross-like and resurrection-like. One cannot claim to be "in Christ," that is, to have in one's experience a Christ-like manifestation of God, if the experience is not also cross-like (see 2 Corinthians 10—13).

4. Paul's attitude, however, is not masochistic. He does not enjoy suffering and does not claim that suffering is a gift from God! For instance, about his "thorn in the flesh" (sickness?) he writes that it is "a messenger from Satan" (2 Cor. 12:7). Similarly, persecutions are by evil people who "displease God and oppose all [people]" (1 Thess. 2:15). In brief, any suffering, and, of course, its ultimate form death, is intrinsically evil. Suffering is the manifestation of "enemies" that Christ is in the process of destroying, and "the last enemy to be destroyed is death" (see 1 Cor. 15:24 – 26). Paul has a realistic view of the Christian life: we are *not yet* at the longed-for time of the Parousia when all suffering and evil will have been defeated.

In brief, Paul does not ask his readers to consider their suffering as a blessing from God. Yet Christ-like manifestations of God in our experience are for Paul necessarily *both* cross-like and resurrection-like. How can this be?

5. Our puzzlement, and apparently, that of the Corinthians, over this apparent contradiction arises from our tendency to look for God's manifestations in the wrong places! We, like the Corinthians, look for and treasure finding God's manifestations in ourselves and in the personal part of our experience. That is, for most of us the *center* of our experience lies in our private and personal experience: a truly religious experience is a private matter. The manifestations of God which are most important are personal experiences which establish us in a personal relationship with God. Thus we look for Christ-like manifestations of God in our personal life.

As long as we hold such a view we cannot understand Paul. Indeed, according to Paul, the *center* of our experience is *in other people* who are also part of our experience since they interact with us. It is in other people that we must first discover Christ-like manifestations of God or manifestations of Christ. It is only through other people that we can be in relationship with God, and then discover true manifestations of God in our personal experience.

This is what Paul succinctly expresses by emphasizing the importance of love. He ranks love above faith: "So faith, hope, and love abide, these three; but the greatest of these is love" (1 Cor. 13:13). For him, love is not the fruit of, or result of faith, but rather faith is the fruit of love. And what is love? The description of love in 1 Corinthians 13 can be summarized by the exhortation: "Consider others as better than yourselves" (Phil. 2:3). As a detailed exegesis of Philippians 2 shows, this means that we should have toward others the same attitude we have toward Christ (see the Greek of Phil. 2:5). Paul does not call us to false humility, pretending that others are better than ourselves, but to true humility which is possible because we see in others Christ-like manifestations. The "others" are not perfect, but in them we can see God manifesting himself to us and calling us (1 Thess. 1:4 – 5). By loving other people, by considering them as better than ourselves, and by looking for the manifestations of God in them, we will discover in them fulfillment of the gospel as promise. Thereby we will be convinced of the truth of the gospel's promise and have faith. Faith is indeed the consequence of love. No wonder that for Paul love is more important than the gifts of the Spirit (see 1 Cor. 12:31), although love itself is the fruit of the Spirit (Gal. 5:22).

6. These observations begin to define one type of situation in which we can expect to discover God at work in our present: situations in which people are both cross-like and resurrection-like. While we can grasp the general principle, we are not yet ready to apply it. We still need to discover in a more specific way how Paul himself applied it. Is any kind of suffering or deprivation cross-like? Is any kind of joy and success resurrection-like? How can a cross-like situation simultaneously be a manifestation of God and of evil? Recognizing, with Paul, that we need to look to others rather than to ourselves to identify Christ-like manifestations will help us address these questions. Nevertheless, to do so we must understand better how Paul viewed the cross and the resurrection as the type of God's manifestations in our experience.

THESIS 7

It is as manifestation of the power of God for the salvation of some of the Jews that the Christ event—cross and resurrection—is the "type" of God's manifestations in our experience.

Notes

1. For Paul, as we have seen, the cross and the resurrection open a new era by inaugurating both the reconciliation of the world to God and the exaltation of Jesus Christ as the Lord. In addition, one needs to note that the cross and the resurrection are also the intervention of God in favor of a specific group of people, the Jews. "When the time had fully come, God sent forth his Son, born of woman, born under the law, to redeem those who were under the law" (Gal. 4:4 – 5). Christ is thereby the "type" of the manifestations of God in the experience of other groups of people. We need therefore to consider carefully Paul's view of the situation of the Jews.

2. Before the coming of Christ the Jews were "under the law," that

is under a "custodian" (Gal. 3:24) as slaves (Galatians 4). Since they relied on works of the Law, they were "under a curse" (Gal. 3:10). In fact, since "the power of sin is the law" (1 Cor. 15:56), being under the Law equals being under the power of sin. This is the situation described in Romans 7. The passage also emphasizes that it is not the Law in and of itself which is evil: "the law is holy, and the commandment is holy and just and good" (Rom. 7:12).

As Paul suggests in Romans 2, the situation of the Jews is comparable to that of the Gentiles. Gentiles had received a true revelation: "For what can be known about God is plain to them, because God has shown it to them. Ever since the creation of the world his invisible nature, namely, his eternal power and deity, has been clearly perceived in the things that have been made" (Rom. 1:19 – 20). But instead of worshiping God they worship *manifestations* of God. In other words, the Gentiles have made an absolute out of the revelation they have received. As a consequence they have been enslaved to their idols (Rom. 1:21 – 32).

The case of the Jews is similar. They have received a revelation, a much more significant revelation (Rom. 3:1 – 2) especially since it includes a revelation of the nature of sin (Rom. 7:7). "To them belong the sonship, the glory, the covenants, the giving of the law, the worship, and the promises" (Rom. 9:4). But this revelation is "veiled" for the Jews. "Their minds were hardened; for to this day, when they read the old covenant, that same veil remains unlifted" (2 Cor. 3:14). The Law has become a curse for them. We can say, using the analogy of the fate of the Gentiles—a correlation that Paul himself makes in Galatians 4—that the Jews have made out of the Law an idol. They have made a complete and final revelation out of a partial revelation, out of a promise. Then, they are trapped in the infernal circle described in Rom. 7:13 – 24. They recognize correctly the Law (Torah) as revelation from God. They correctly want to serve God, but as they proceed to do so, they do the very thing they hate. By following the Law which has been transformed into an idol, they are in fact idolatrous. Instead of serving the living God, the God of the promises, they serve a god limited to past revelations. So, the more they strive to serve their god, the true God enclosed in past revelations, the more they sin against God. They have confused minds. What they take to be good may indeed be good, perhaps a part of the true revelation, but it might also be evil; a good defined by their idolatry, by their sin, is in fact an evil. And what they take to be evil might indeed be evil, as defined by God, but might also be good; it might be a sin as defined by their sin, their idolatry. As the Gentiles are under a curse, so are they. The Law, the true revelation of God, has become for them the power of sin. Such is, for Paul, the situation of the Jews under the Law.

3. The act of redemption, the manifestation of the power of God for the salvation of some of the Jews, unfolds in several stages.

a. God sends his Son to the Jews. Christ "emptied himself, taking the form of a servant [slave], being born in the likeness of men. And being found in human form he humbled himself and became obedient unto death, even death on a cross" (Phil. 2:7 – 8). In Paul's own words, he became "Jew with the Jews." But, of course, Christ did not participate in their sin (2 Cor. 5:21). As a consequence he refuses to do the "good as defined by their sinful view of the law," since it is in fact sin, and does the "evil as defined by their sinful view of the law" since it is in fact good. So from the perspective of the sinful Jews, Jesus appears to be sinful. He is a sinful human being or sinful flesh according to, or from the perspective of, the Jews' sin. This is what Paul expresses in Rom. 8:3: "[God] sending his own Son in the likeness of sinful flesh *according to* sin" (au. trans.). One can then understand what Paul writes in 2 Cor. 5:21: "he [God] made him [Christ] to be sin who knew no sin."

b. As a consequence, the Jews reject Jesus as a sinful, blasphemous person and they crucify him (1 Thess. 2:15). The crucifixion demonstrates that he is cursed, "for it is written, 'Cursed be every one who hangs on a tree' " (Gal. 3:13). Yet note that Paul does not say that it is the true God who cursed Jesus. In fact, he is not truly cursed, that is, cursed by God, as Paul emphasizes in 1 Cor. 12:2 – 3. Only when one is "led astray to dumb idols," when one is an idolater, can one say that Jesus is cursed.

It is now clear how the cross is a manifestation of God. It is not God who brings about suffering, who punishes, and who curses Jesus, but rather the Jews as slaves of their idolatry to the Law. God intervenes sending his faithful Son into the sinful situation; a situation in which the Son can only be rejected, persecuted, and killed in the name of the idol. The Jews believe that in crucifying Jesus they are zealously serving God, "but [their zeal] is not enlightened" (Rom. 10:2).

c. Following Christ's death the Jews are still slaves of their idol, the Law. But the story does not end with the cross. Christ is "designated [literally, "marked out," "manifested as"] Son of God in power according to the Spirit of holiness by his resurrection from the dead" (Rom. 1:4). He appears to Cephas, to the Twelve, to more than five hundred people, and to James (1 Cor. 15:4 – 7). For all the Jews Jesus was rightfully (or so they thought) crucified because he was a sinner. But when some of them discover that Jesus has been raised from the dead and thus has been shown by God to be righteous, then it is a clear demonstration that their faith is wrong. They can recognize their faith for what it is: the power of sin which holds them in bondage, under a curse. The power of this curse is broken. They are free. The veil has been lifted (2 Cor. 3:16 – 17). They have eyes which can see. "For freedom Christ set [them] free" (Gal. 5:1). They can share in the glorious liberty of the children of God (Rom. 8:21) and receive the spirit of sonship (Rom. 8:15).

4. It is as manifestation of the power of God for the salvation of [some of] the Jews that the Christ event—cross and resurrection—is the "type" of God's manifestations after that time. Because of his conviction that the Christ event effected the reconciliation of the world to God, Paul can perceive it, through faith, as the promise and, more specifically, the "type" of God's manifestations in our own experience. Using the Christ event as the lens through which he looks at everything around him ("from now on, therefore, we regard no one from a human point of view," 2 Cor. 5:16), Paul can then perceive how God is at work in his present situation.

We can distinguish several kinds of situations to which Paul applies this type: (1) situations of conversion; (2) situations of believers fulfilling their vocation—the church as body of Christ; (3) other situations which can be more clearly perceived when one takes into account the ultimate fulfillment which Paul hopes for at the Parousia. I will examine them separately (in Theses 8, 9, and 10, respectively), since each kind of situation involves the fulfillment of the gospel we will have to proclaim.

THESIS 8

The Christ event—cross and resurrection—as type is most directly
fulfilled in the situation of conversion. Conversion occurs only
when someone is sent by God into the world of the idolaters/sinners,
is rejected by them (as Christ was sent in sinful flesh and crucified),
and is manifested to them as sent by God through a resurrection-like
manifestation of God. Thus, it is in people who are at first incor-
rectly perceived as sinners that one can discover Christ-like manifestations of God.

Notes

1. We can recognize a Christ-like manifestation of God, a manifestation of the power of the gospel, each time we see someone or
several people sent by God into the sinful world. Because the people
who are sent are faithful to God, they are rejected and persecuted
by the sinners in the name of their "faith" and their "righteousness,"
both alleged to be false. These messengers of God are "unrighteous"
people according to the sinners' idolatry. But then God demonstrates that his messengers are in fact righteous by intervening in a
resurrection-like way. These resurrection-like manifestations of
God vary, and indeed need to vary. They are necessarily related to
the kinds of revelation that the sinners have received and transformed into idols. Otherwise the sinners would not be able to recognize these "resurrection-like" manifestations of God as truly from
God.

2. In the case of Paul's "conversion" we find all these elements.
The church was the Christ-like group for Paul. He, a zealous and
righteous Pharisee, found the church to be blasphemous, rejected
it, and persecuted it (1 Cor. 15:9; Gal. 1:13 – 14; Phil. 3:5 – 6). It is
not by chance that Paul mentions his persecution of the church each
time he speaks of his conversion. The church as persecuted by Paul is
cross-like for him. But then, there is a resurrection-like manifestation of God, indeed, a manifestation of the risen Christ. Thus Paul
discovers that it is "the church of God" that he is persecuting (Gal.
1:13), and not a group of blasphemers. This discovery demonstrates
to him that his "zeal" for God and his "righteousness under the law"
which led him to persecute the church are in fact "a loss" (Phil.

3:5 – 9). Through this cross-like and resurrection-like manifestation of God, Paul is freed from the bondage of the Law in which he was trapped (Gal. 3:23—4:7). Note that he has received faith because he has first recognized God at work in other people: it was the church of God that he persecuted (Gal. 1:13; 1 Cor. 15:9).

Paul the Jew was converted by a Christ-like manifestation of God after Christ's death and resurrection. Yet it seems that Paul viewed his own conversion as an exceptional case because it involved an appearance of the resurrected Christ comparable to that of Cephas, the Twelve, the five hundred, and James (1 Cor. 15:5 – 10).

3. Other Jews, indeed most of the Jews, still needed to be converted. Paul explains his missionary strategy toward the Jews in Rom. 11:13 – 14. He "magnifies" his ministry among the Gentiles so as to make the Jews jealous. We can now understand what this means. For the Jews, Gentiles who do not follow the Law are by definition sinners (Gal. 2:15). They must be despised and rejected. But, by "magnifying" his ministry, Paul is trying to point out to the Jews that the converted Gentiles, even though they do not follow the Law—according to Paul's Gospel they are free from the Law—are now serving the true God, the God of Israel. In other words, he attempts to show the Jews that the Gentiles' conversion from idolatry is the work of God. In this way Paul hopes to make the Jews "jealous," that is, to shock them into abandoning their "idolatrous" faith in the Law (Torah). Ultimately they will convert, Paul hopes, when they recognize God at work among the despised Gentiles.

4. In turn, Paul is the person in whom Gentiles such as the Corinthians recognize God at work. He becomes Greek with the Greeks; he enters their sinful world (1 Cor. 9:21). But, by refusing to teach a wisdom, by not being a good speaker, and by working with his hands, he "sins" against their Greek idolatry which valued "wisdom," "rhetoric," and "social status" (1 Corinthians 1—2, 4). Such is his ministry which cannot but be rejected by the wise and noble Corinthians. In this way, he is cross-like for them. But then, in his ministry, God intervenes "in demonstration of the Spirit and of power" (1 Cor. 2:4). These resurrection-like manifestations in the midst of his "weak" ministry—blasphemy to the Corinthians as Greek idolaters—are the basis of the Corinthians' faith. Thus, once more, it is by discovering God's manifestations in someone else—

Paul and his ministry—that the Corinthians receive faith and are freed from their idolatry.

5. Let me emphasize: It is always by discovering God at work in someone whom we hold to be a sinner, that we can be freed from our idolatry, whatever it may be. Recognizing God at work in our private experiences cannot free us from idolatry. The same is true of recognizing God's manifestations only in people whom we view as good. To begin with, what is recognized as a "manifestation of God" might not be from God; it might be a manifestation of our idol, which, of course, we consider to be God. More importantly, even if we have identified a true manifestation of God, such a recognition can only have the effect of convincing us even more that we are right and thereby righteous. Instead of freeing us from our idolatry, the attitude of constantly looking for and recognizing divine manifestations in our private experiences and/or in people whom we view as good reinforces our idolatry. Let's not pretend that we are not idolaters. Paul insists that "none is righteous, no, not one" (Rom. 3:10). In fact, the very attitude of looking exclusively for God's manifestations in our own private experiences and in those we view as good people is a sign that we are trapped in bondage to some kind of idolatry. Only when we recognize God's manifestation in people whom we view as "sinners," no-goods, foolish, the "refuse of the world" (1 Cor. 4:13) can we recognize the true manifestations of God in our private experiences, be freed from our idolatry and be prevented from making new idols out of the gifts we receive from God.

6. If we are not only to convert and receive faith but also to keep that faith, to walk in faith rather than backsliding into a new idolatry, we must look for God's manifestations among people we consider to be sinners, people whom we despise, whom we view as foolish and as "refuse of the world." Similarly, if our preaching is to convert non-believers and nurture the faith of believers, it will need to "magnify" how God intervenes in people whom our hearers—and we, at first—consider sinful, despicable, and foolish. Such a preaching will be controversial, even foolish. It should not however be foolish for the sake of foolishness. We will not find in all sinners resurrection-like manifestations of God. There are many sinners

who are truly sinners, rather than merely appearing to be sinners.[11] But the promise of reconciliation means that there are always Christ-like people around us. Through them we can be set free from any idolatry in which we are trapped, or from any potential idolatry that waits to enslave us once more.

THESIS 9

The Christ event—cross and resurrection—as type is also fulfilled in believers who faithfully carry out their vocation. In fact, it is their vocation to offer themselves "as a living sacrifice" so as to become an occasion for the manifestation of the power of the gospel for the salvation of others.

Notes

1. Paul explains the vocation of the believers most clearly in Rom. 12:1 – 2:

> I appeal to you therefore, brethren, by the mercies of God, to present your bodies as a living sacrifice, holy and acceptable, which is your spiritual worship. Do not be conformed to this world but transformed by the renewal of your mind, that you may prove [or, "test", i.e., "discover by testing"] what is the will of God, what is good and acceptable and perfect.

Paul's self-example shows what is involved in offering oneself as a living sacrifice. It is becoming a Jew with Jews, a Greek with Greeks, weak with the weak, and so forth (1 Cor. 9:19 – 23). It is becoming Christ-like for others by entering their sinful and idolatrous world. Yet, of course, all that the believers can do is to accept being sent into the sinful world of other people, and to act therein as faithful and obedient servants of God as Christ did (Phil. 2:7 – 8). They cannot conform themselves to the sinful world. They must act in a way which appears to be sinful, despicable, and improper to people who belong to that world. As such they can expect to be rejected, despised, and even persecuted—as Christ was, and as Paul also was (see again 1 Corinthians 1—4). But they can have courage

11. See the discussion of "sinners who are truly sinners, rather than merely appearing to be sinners" as it is applied to contemporary situations in Thesis 14, Note 3(b).

to do so (1 Thess. 2:2) because they can trust the promise and thus hope for God's manifestation in a resurrection-like fashion. Since it is by obedience to God who sends them that they have entered the world of sinners and find themselves "crucified" or in a cross-like situation, then they can confidently hope that God will intervene in a resurrection-like fashion. There is of course no guarantee that the intervention of God will necessarily be in their favor, saving them from death at the hands of their persecutors, for instance. Resurrection-like interventions of God aim at manifesting the power of God so that, at least, some of these people may be saved (Phil. 1:12 – 26).

2. In most instances, believers are called to enter or simply to remain in the sinful world from which they converted. Recall the common exhortation of Paul which applies to all aspects of the believers' life, and which can be summarized in the motto, "Remain as you are." "This is my rule in all the churches . . . Every one should remain in the state in which he was called" (1 Cor. 7:17, 20; see 7:17 – 24). Thus Gentiles should remain Gentiles, and consequently continue to lead a Hellenistic way of life, and not a Jewish way of life following the Law (Torah), as far as is possible without betraying the gospel (see Galatians). Similarly, Paul agrees that Jews can, and should, follow a Jewish way of life and thus the Law, as far as is possible without betraying the gospel (Gal. 2:7 – 9). But, of course, as believers, they are Greeks with the Greeks or Jews with the Jews while, at the same time, being free from the idolatry of the Greeks or from the "idolatry" of the Jews, that is, faith in Torah as a complete and final revelation. As such believers are cross-like in two ways: on the one hand, they are rejected, despised, persecuted; on the other hand, they demonstrate that "they have died to" their former idolatry, that is, that they have been "crucified with Christ" (Gal. 2:20) which, in the case of Paul, means that he "died to the Law" (Gal. 2:19).

3. Paul's discussion of the incident at Antioch helps us understand how the believers can remain as they are, participating in their former idolatrous world even though they have died to it. At Jerusalem, what is right in Peter's as well as in James' and John's attitude is that, while they continue to preach a gospel with the

Law, they accept the validity of the gospel without the Law that Paul preaches. Consequently, Peter does not consider as an absolute either his form of the gospel or the Law. By contrast, at Antioch, Peter's attitude demonstrates that he considers as an absolute, or at least as an ideal, the gospel *with* the Law. For Paul, dying to the Law means to give it up as an absolute which one has to follow in order to be in right relationship with God (Gal. 2:11 – 21). In other words, dying to the Law or dying to one of the Hellenistic religions is to reject it as idolatry, that is, as a religion which has made an absolute out of something which is not an absolute. This does not mean that there is nothing good in these religions. In fact, as we shall see in our discussion of Thesis 11, for Paul, any idolatry involves a true revelation. Consequently, believers entering a world of idolatry need, on the one hand, to avoid being conformed to this world and being idolatrous with it. On the other hand, they must discern what is "the will of God, what is good and acceptable and perfect" in the idolatrous world, for indeed, this should not be rejected. Thus the believers who offer themselves as a living sacrifice need to "test everything," "prove" what is good in this idolatrous world (Rom. 12:2).

4. From the preceding remarks it follows that our preaching needs to proclaim the fulfillment of the gospel as manifested in those who offer themselves as a living sacrifice. In a faithful community, we can preach "thanksgiving sermons." But, through our preaching, we also need to offer ourselves as a living sacrifice (see Thesis 8, Note 6).

THESIS 10

The church as a community of believers who "consider others as better than themselves" and "offer themselves as a living sacrifice" is the "body of Christ," a fulfillment of the Christ event—cross and resurrection—as type.

Notes

1. For Paul, individual believers cannot, by definition, carry out their vocation as individuals. Faith necessarily involves discovering

God at work in other people who have been cross-like and resurrection-like for us. This is not only true at the time of conversion when we are freed from our idolatry but also remains true afterward because of our humanity. We have been freed from *a power of sin*, our idolatry, but not from *sin* itself. Sin is dormant in the believers, it "lies dead" (Rom. 7:8), but at any moment it can revive, finding opportunity in something good received from God (as it found opportunity in the "holy and just and good" commandment, Rom. 7:8 – 12). In order to ward off the ever present danger of being enslaved once more to a power of sin, we constantly need to recognize in other people Christ-like manifestations. We need to "consider others as better than ourselves" (Phil. 2:3), an attitude which is nothing other than love (1 Corinthians 13).

Constantly recognizing Christ-like manifestations in others requires us to acknowledge that God is continually working to free us from actual and potential bondages. For such a liberation, a community of believers cannot but constantly be giving thanks. A community of believers will constantly be celebrating the passover, deliverance from bondage. "For Christ, our paschal [passover] lamb, has been sacrificed. Let us, therefore, celebrate the festival" (1 Cor. 5:7 – 8).

2. The very fact that a community constantly gives thanks for Christ-like manifestations shows that it is being freed from idolatries and thus from the marks of idolatry which are destructive attitudes, among which is immorality in its various forms (1 Corinthians 5—6 and Rom. 1:18 – 32)

3. I do not mean to say that the church only includes "strong" believers. There are also "weak" believers. But then the strong believers need to carry out their vocation toward these weak believers as they also do toward outsiders (see 1 Cor. 8:1 – 11:1). Yet weak believers can still be "loved," or, in other words, "considered as better than ourselves." They have received gifts from God which we have not received, gifts that we need to receive through them. The recognition of the God given gifts of weak believers is necessary so that believers may become Christ-like for others.

4. Such is a community of believers that is the body of Christ. Fulfilling its vocation among "insiders" and toward "outsiders," the

community—as well as its individual members—offers itself as a living sacrifice. The believers accept the call to be cross-like, poor, rejected, persecuted. But the church is also the place where God's gifts and the Spirit's gifts are manifested in a privileged way. In other words, it is also the community in which God manifests his power for salvation through resurrection-like manifestations. The believers, however, need to keep in mind that God's gifts are resurrection-like manifestations *for others* and not for themselves, as the Corinthians mistakenly thought (1 Corinthians 12—14). These gifts are given to the church as it carries out its vocation by offering itself as a living sacrifice.

5. The gifts that the faithful community as body of Christ receives as it fulfills its vocation are, therefore, a fulfillment of the promise of the Gospel. Our preaching can and in fact needs to celebrate these resurrection-like gifts. Yet, it must carefully relate them to the vocation of the church. In other words, these gifts have to be celebrated as God's manifestations for others, and not for ourselves. They are given to us only as we become cross-like by entering the idolatrous world of other people. Therefore, it is when we are powerless that these gifts are given to us so that we might manifest for others the power of God (2 Cor. 12:9, 1 Cor. 2:3 – 5). Our preaching will be a true celebration of God's gifts only when it is simultaneously a demonstration of our powerlessness.

THESIS 11

Paul envisions the end of time—the time of the Parousia—as a further fulfillment of the Christ event beyond its fulfillment in the believers' experience. Consequently, the situations which can be viewed as prefigurations of the eschatological interventions of God can in turn be identified by the believers as manifestations of God in their present.

Notes

1. The fulfillment of the Christ event in the experience of believers involves a diversity of manifestations of the power of God for their salvation. In the present believers have been saved (freed) from

their bondage to the power of sin, from their bondage to the Law as a manifestation of the power of sin, or from their bondage to various idols as other manifestations of the power of sin. Being freed is a resurrection-like experience, but is not complete salvation. Any manifestation of God's power in the believers' experience, despite its great importance, is merely the promise, the type, of the ultimate manifestation of God's power at the Parousia. Believers have in their present experience *resurrection-like* manifestations of God such as the "joy inspired by the Spirit" (1 Thess. 1:6) or being freed from sin (1 Cor. 15:17). At the Parousia, however, they will be raised from the dead and to heaven just as Christ was (1 Thess. 4:13 – 18). The manifestations of God that believers discover in their experience, through faith, are the ground for their hope.

2. Since the experience of believers is, for Paul, the fulfillment of the type of the Christ event, it is also the "prefiguration" or the "preliminary manifestation" of the eschatological situation. Consequently, one can identify other interventions of God in the present by looking for the prefigurations or preliminary manifestations of other kinds of divine intervention at the time of the Parousia. I will consider two particularly important cases so as to clarify the easily misunderstood concept of "prefiguration of divine manifestation." Of course we need to keep in mind that, for Paul, a situation is truly a prefiguration of the future divine manifestation only insofar as it can also be viewed as fulfillment of the type of the Christ event.

a. Christ was crucified by the "Jews" (1 Thess. 2:14 – 15), or more precisely, by the Jews under the bondage of the Law, which is the power of sin. Consequently, Paul can say that, in fact, Christ was crucified by evil powers, "the rulers of this age" (1 Cor. 2:8, also called "authorities" and "powers" in 1 Cor. 15:24). Believers are despised, rejected, persecuted by the Jews or by fellow-citizens who are under the power of sin (1 Thess. 2:14) and in whom evil powers are manifested. Similarly, at the end of time there will be a manifestation of a destructive power which is nothing else than the "wrath of God" (1 Thess. 1:10; see 2:16; 5:1 – 11).

The crucifixion of Christ *and* the persecution of the believers are therefore "prefigurations" or preliminary manifestations of the wrath of God which will destroy all evil at the end of time.

Paul expresses the relationship of the crucifixion, the persecution of the believers, and the eschatological judgment and destruction in Rom. 1:18 – 32. Idolaters, that is, the people who are described elsewhere as being "slaves to the elemental spirits of the universe" (evil powers comparable to the "rulers of this age," Gal. 4:3,9), are here described as being under the wrath of God. Consequently, according to Paul, believers should identify as interventions of God in their present, both manifestations of God's "power for salvation" and manifestations of God's "wrath" (Rom. 1:16 – 18).

Gentiles are in bondage to idols they made for themselves, and thus, they are responsible for their idolatry and "without excuse" (Rom. 1:20). Nevertheless these idols have power over them. They are manifestations of the power of sin, of evil powers. While these powers are enemies of God and of Christ (1 Cor. 15:24 – 25), they are simultaneously manifestations of the wrath of God. It is God who "gave (the idolaters) up" to the power of their idols (Rom. 1:24,26,28). As the manifestation of the wrath of God at the end of time will be destructive, so is the manifestation of the wrath of God for the idolaters in the present. Given up "in the lusts of their hearts to impurity" (Rom. 1:24), "to dishonorable passions" (Rom. 1:26), and "to a base mind and to improper conduct" (Rom. 1:28) they destroy themselves and all human relationship. The case of the Jews is similar. Their bondage to the Law leads them to death (Rom. 7:10). In sum, idolatry, whatever the idol, is a manifestation of the wrath of God.

Yet Paul is not a prophet of wrath. He proclaims the good news of the gospel. Manifestations of the wrath of God also are manifestations of the enemies which keep human beings in bondage and which are being destroyed by Christ as Lord. Identification of the manifestation of the wrath of God is not, therefore, for the purpose of self-righteously proclaiming a message of condemnation. "Therefore you have no excuse, O man, whoever you are, when you judge another; for in passing judgment upon him you condemn yourself" (Rom. 2:1). Yet such identification is important for the fulfillment of one's vocation as a believer (see Thesis 9).

b. By obedience to God, Christ was sent in the likeness of sinful flesh (Rom. 8:3), that is, he became a slave (Phil. 2:7) of the idolatrous powers. He was under their power and was put to death by them. By fulfilling their vocation and offering themselves as a living sacrifice, believers enter the world of the idolaters and submit themselves to the idolatrous powers.

Both in the case of Christ and the case of the believers "something" good (people sent by God) which was under the power of the idolatrous powers is delivered and vindicated by an intervention of God. Similarly, creation, the good creation of God, is enslaved to idolatrous powers and "has been groaning in travail . . . until now" (Rom. 8:22). The Law which is holy, just, and good, in which sin found opportunity, is veiled "to this day" (1 Cor. 3:14), and in bondage to sin. Both the creation and the Law are described by Paul as true revelations from God (Rom. 1:20 on creation; Rom. 3:2, and throughout Romans on the Law), which have been enslaved to sin and transformed into idols. But at the Parousia they will be freed from bondage and vindicated, appearing for what they really are: true revelations of God. Read what Paul says about creation in Rom. 8:19 – 21:

> For the creation waits with eager longing for the revealing of the sons of God; for the creation was subjected to futility, not of its own will but by the will of him who subjected it in hope; because the creation itself will be set free from its bondage to decay and obtain the glorious liberty of the children of God.

Similarly, the Law was subjected to futility and veiled because of sin (Rom. 7:8), though for believers the veil is lifted by the Lord (2 Cor. 3:14 – 18). And, even though Paul does not say so explicitly, we can assume that this veil will be totally lifted at the Parousia.

There are, therefore, four main manifestations of God that believers can recognize in their experience when they no longer look at it "from a human point of view" but rather look at it from the point of view of reconciliation (1 Cor. 5:16 – 19).

1. Believers are able to recognize that *in each idolatry there is a true revelation from God:* creation as revelation of God's "invisible nature, namely his eternal power and deity" (Rom. 1:20) in the idolatries of the Gentiles; the Law as "the oracles of God" (Rom. 3:2) in the "idolatry" of the Jews.

2. Believers are able to identify this true revelation of God in each idolatry because they can distinguish it from another manifestation of God, the manifestation of *wrath* which is also to be found in each idolatry.

3. Believers are able to recognize God's manifestations in the experience of being freed from the bondage to a power of sin, their idolatry. For Paul such manifestations of God are necessarily Christ-like. God frees sinners and idolaters from their bondage through other people who, at first, appear to be sinners to the future believers. Consequently, as Christ was crucified, these other people are righteously rejected by the future believers, but God demonstrates that these people are actually his servants through a resurrection-like manifestation.

4. Finally, believers are able to recognize that God has intervened when they can truly benefit from and receive the gifts of God and of his Spirit. To begin with, when they are freed from the bondage to their idolatries, they have access to the true revelation which was "veiled" or imprisoned in their idolatries. Torah is again the life-giving word (2 Cor. 3:4 – 18), and creation is again the manifestation of God's "eternal power and deity" (Rom. 1:20). They also receive gifts of the Spirit. But all these gifts are given to them for the benefit of others. These are resurrection-like manifestations and prefigurations of the eschatological blessings through which God makes them Christ-like as they offer themselves as a living sacrifice and thus accept to be cross-like. God's manifestation in a community of such believers transforms this community into the body of Christ.

3
Proclaiming the Gospel as Power of God for Salvation

Now it is time to elaborate on what preaching should be if we truly want to transmit the faith of the gospel which Paul proclaimed.

Our preaching needs to have the following characteristics:

First, it needs to proclaim *the kerygma and Paul's teaching as a promise.* Such a presentation of the *kerygma* and of Paul's teaching can be relatively straightforward—a descriptive presentation, that is, a simple retelling of the story. There is no need for elaborate explanatory and argumentative developments as long as it is clearly presented as a promise, and not as a complete and final revelation.

Second, our preaching needs to make clear the content of the promise. The reconciliation of the world to God in Jesus Christ is the promise that, in our present, *sinners are being freed from the powers of sin,* or that idolaters are freed from the bondage to their idolatries, through Christ-like manifestations. This is the good news of the gospel, and indeed all that we need from God, regardless of what we think.

Third, our preaching needs to be *a preaching of the church to the church.* In other words, it needs to point out to the church the Christ-like manifestations of God in the church—in certain of its members, in certain of its groups that are both cross-like and resurrection-like for the rest of a congregation or of the church at large. This is a call to faithfulness, a call to grow in faith by seeing others as better than ourselves, a call to be a truly loving community, and also a call to celebration. Such a church can thus be a community constantly celebrating the Passover by giving thanks to God for interventions that believers can recognize in each other.

Fourth, our preaching needs to be *a preaching of the world* (sic!) *to the church* which is both a call to repentance and a call to mission in the world. On the one hand, our preaching needs to proclaim the Christ-like manifestations of God in the world in which the Lord precedes us. These manifestations are both a call to repentance—by pointing out that we have let ourselves be imprisoned in our church routines—and a call to mission, that is, a call to join the Lord in his action. On the other hand, our preaching needs to proclaim what is from God, that which is truly good, in the secular and idolatrous world, while pointing out what are the urgent needs of the world. In so doing we need to suggest ways in which one can offer oneself as a living sacrifice for this world in confident hope that God will use us to save at least a few (1 Cor. 9:22) by intervening in a resurrection-like fashion. Then we are on mission in the world.

Such preaching might be and almost certainly will be rejected by certain members of the church and at times by entire congregations who will feel threatened, if they have turned the gospel into an idol which gives them a feeling of peace and security while it destroys them. By such prophetic preaching we make ourselves cross-like for our congregation. Our sermons embody the message of the cross. We are perceived to be unreasonable (1 Cor. 2:4; see 1:18 – 31) by pointing out that God is at work in places where, for many, God is obviously not at work, and by neglecting to point out that God is at work in people who are perceived as good. But if we do so with humility, with the faith which allows us to see others as better than ourselves, we can hope that God will also intervene in a resurrection-like manner in the congregation and through our preaching. Our preaching will be "not only in word, but also in power and in the Holy Spirit and with full conviction" (1 Thess. 1:5).

THESIS 12

The proclamation of the kerygma and of Paul's teaching as a prom-ise, a necessary part of our preaching, can be simply descriptive: a retelling of the story. There is no need to demonstrate the validity and truth of the message by means of elaborate explanations, as if the proof of its validity and truth resided in the message itself and in the events of the biblical time it reports. The validity and truth of a PROMISE are most directly established by the discovery of the FULFILLMENT of that promise.

Notes

1. In our preaching we are often concerned to bridge, for our hearers, the cultural and historical gap which separates us from Paul's teaching and the *kerygma*. His message is indeed linked to an outdated religious world which has very little in common with the contemporary Western world in which we carry out our ministries. We are no longer in a world in which the major issue for the church is to know whether the Law needs to be carried out as it was in Judaism; in a society in which the majority of unbelievers worship cosmological idols; in an apocalyptically minded culture in which a large section of the population is expecting the wrathful judgment of God at any time; or even in a culture expecting truly transcendent manifestations of God. The "transcendent" manifestations of our God, or god, are now limited in practice to the personal and private dimensions of our individual lives, that is, to what Dietrich Bonhoeffer would call a "corner of our lives." We live in a culture and world in which a description of the gospel as "the power of God freeing sinners from the power of sin" is bound to be misunderstood as God's manifestations in the private life of an individual, simply because we are so deeply convinced that sin is primarily a matter concerning our inner self. How then can we understand how Paul relates sin to cosmic evil powers such as the "elemental spirits of the universe," the "rulers of this world," the "authorities?"

2. We are confronting the problem that Rudolf Bultmann addressed by suggesting that the task of preaching involves us in "demythologizing," that is, in "translating" given cultural views so as to express those views in a symbolism attuned to the culture of our hearers. An interpretation aimed at bridging the historical gap which separates the biblical text from modern people, a hermeneutic, is indeed necessary. For preaching Paul—transmitting the faith Paul proclaimed—this hermeneutic should not, however, be a demythologization.

Demythologization is needed only if the faith to be communicated is defined as follows: believing and trusting a message about
God's decisive and "once and for all" manifestations in the past, so
that one can appropriate the benefit of these manifestations. In the
case of this common understanding of faith, the essential thing is
the communication of the message, of a knowledge. The appropria-
tion of this faith by modern people rests then on the preacher's ability to present the message in such a way that it may be understood
and perceived as true. Proofs of the truth of the message are pre-
sumed to be in the message itself. Preaching is then expounding the
message in order to demonstrate its inherent truth by showing the
meaning of its vocabulary and symbolism, and by re-expressing it in
modern terms. In such an understanding of faith and preaching,
demythologization is imperative.

Yet this is *not* the kind of preaching demanded by Paul's gospel.
In brief, since the message of the gospel is a *promise*, proofs of its
truth lie not in the message itself, but in its fulfillment. If people
see this fulfillment, they will be convinced of the validity of the
message/promise.

3. If Paul's gospel is promise, the cultural gap which separates
us from his vocabulary and symbolism is no longer the main issue.
The problem of interpretation can be addressed in a quite different way. In fact, Paul had to face a similar situation as ours
when he went proclaiming the gospel in the Hellenistic world.
The *kerygma*, the message about Jesus Christ, was as foreign to
the Hellenistic people as Paul's teaching is to our culture. At first,
these people certainly understood Paul's words, but without being
able to appropriate the message fully because these words and concepts were not their own. The *kerygma* was fundamentally Jewish.
It announced that Jesus was the Messiah, a Jewish notion, because
he was the fulfillment of the prophecies and promises of the Law
(Torah), the Jewish Scripture. Paul described the manifestation of
God in Christ in terms of sin(s), a Jewish concept directly related
to the Law, and in terms of resurrection, also a Jewish notion that
Hellenistic people could misunderstand because they believed in
the immortality of the soul. The significance of Christ's death for
our sins and resurrection was expressed by means of Jewish (e.g.,

apocalyptic) notions concerning the "day of the Lord," and its imminent coming.

What did Paul do when he proclaimed this *kerygma* to the Gentiles? Quite clearly he preached the *kerygma* in the Jewish terminology in which it was framed. He taught them the Jewish Scripture, its prophecies and promises, and how these were fulfilled in Christ. He explained the *kerygma* to them, as he did in his letters, but without giving up the Jewish vocabulary and concepts. Of course, he used their language, Greek, and quoted the Greek translation of the Hebrew Bible (the Septuagint). Also he was helped by his hearers' acquaintance with Jewish communities of the diaspora. Many of his hearers may even have had direct contacts with Judaism. But this does not mean that they truly understood this Jewish terminology since they conducted their daily lives in a Hellenistic culture in a quite different conceptual world.

Our situation is essentially the same. Most people in our culture are acquainted with the biblical language, even though it may be meaningless for them because they conduct their daily lives in a technological culture which involves a quite different conceptual world. Consequently, as Paul repeated a *kerygma* expressed in Jewish garb to his Gentile audiences, so we can repeat it and Paul's teaching in the outdated language in which it is expressed. The task of interpretation does not concern the presentation of the *kerygma in and of itself.*

The proclamation of the gospel also involves the proclamation of the fulfillment of the *kerygma* as promise and type. In order to understand the interpretation which is needed, it is enough to note the ways in which Paul proceeds. Each time Paul mentions the fulfillment of the gospel in the experience of his readers, he does so *in the vocabulary of his readers.* For instance, he speaks of slavery to the "elemental spirits of the universe" (Gal. 4:3), and of being delivered from "the present evil age [eon]" (Gal. 1:4). Thus he interprets the fulfillment of the Christ event to the Galatians who believed in cosmological powers. In his proclamation of the gospel, therefore, Paul shows to his readers the relationship between their experience and the Jews' experience. The Jews "confined under the law" were sinful (Gal. 3:22 – 23), and the Galatians were enslaved to the "elemental spirits of the universe." Christ freed the Jews from the bondage to the Law (see Gal. 4:5, and throughout), he "gave himself for [their] sins," and Christ freed the Galatians from their bondage to the elemental spirits (that is, "the evil eon"). Consequently, Paul summarizes his proclamation to the Galatians by speaking of "our Lord Jesus Christ, who gave himself for our sins to deliver us from the present evil age [eon]" (Gal. 1:3 – 4).

Paul's proclamation of the gospel therefore involves both repetition of the *kerygma in its Jewish vocabulary,* and a declaration to his hearers and readers of its fulfillment *in terms of their own experience.* The interpretation involved is not one which relates concepts, symbols, and world views of one culture to those of another. Rather, it is an interpretation which relates events, sequences of events, and the situations resulting from these events found in one cultural context to events, sequences of events, and their results as found in another cultural context. (I use the term "event" with the specific meaning of whatever *happens* to people and *affects* them, their life, their view of life, and their view of the world.)

What does this mean for our own preaching? Even though we will need to relate the experience of our contemporaries to Paul's message and its vocabulary, it is essential that we first describe what *happens* in their experience *in the very vocabulary they themselves are using* to speak about it. This is necessary even though we will have discovered what truly happens in our contemporaries' experience by looking at it through the lens of the *kerygma* and of Paul's teaching. Consequently, it is totally useless to speak at first of our contemporaries' "bondage to the power of sin." They would understand the words but totally misunderstand them because of their "introspective view of sin."[12] Similarly, it is useless to speak of their "idolatry" and of "their bondage to an idol." They cannot but misunderstand these phrases because they view idolatry as a superstition which can be easily overcome by education, rather than as a bondage from which one cannot hope to escape without a divine intervention. By contrast, the proclamation of the gospel to our contemporaries demands that we first identify what keeps people in

12. See Krister Stendahl, "The Apostle Paul and the Introspective Conscience of the West," in *Paul Among Jews and Gentiles* (Philadelphia: Fortress Press, 1976), 78 – 96.

bondage in the present and point it out to them. (For instance, during the Nazi period one needed to show the Germans that they were mesmerized by Nazi propaganda.) Then, and only then, we can show people that their bondage is like the Jew's bondage to the Law as power of sin and like the Gentile's bondage to idols.

Obviously, the preceding remarks do not intend to express fully all that is involved in transmitting the gospel. If our preaching were nothing more it would fail. These remarks merely point out what is essential: when we speak about fulfillment of the gospel, we must do so in terms of the experience in which it is found so that our hearers will have no difficulty identifying it. It is through this fulfillment that people today will be able to grasp the actual meaning of the "strange" phrases of the *kerygma* itself. There is, therefore, no need to make a special effort to explain or even to demythologize the *kerygma in and of itself*. Certainly, our proclamation of it, without demythologization, will at first seem foolish. But our foolishness will make sense for our hearers when they discover, thanks to the rest of our preaching, the fulfillment of the gospel in their own experience (1 Cor. 1:18—2:5).

In the proclamation of Paul's gospel a preacher does not have the responsibility of proving the truth of the message—God does it. The preacher's primary responsibility is to witness to God's fulfillment of the gospel.

THESIS 13

Preaching Paul's gospel is essentially the proclamation that the power of God for salvation is at work in our present, freeing sinners from the power of sin which enslaves them, freeing idolaters from the bondage to their idolatries. For Paul, preaching such a gospel was an urgent and compelling vocation that he needed to carry out relentlessly before it was too late, because of "the wrath to come." So it should be for us.

Notes

1. Thesis 13 leaves us uneasy because it suggests that it is urgent for us to proclaim freedom from the power of sin. Is not Paul's sense of urgency directly related to a first century apocalyptic mindset

and to an eschatological consciousness expecting the end of time in the very near future?

Clearly such was the case for Paul. Yet one should keep in mind the way in which Paul perceived the relation between the last judgment *and* bondage to the power of sin or to idolatry. For him, both are manifestations of the "wrath of God," even though the latter is a preliminary manifestation and the former the ultimate manifestation. While it may be difficult for us to find motivation for our ministry in apocalyptic views, we can be motivated by considering the dreadful consequences of the power of sin and of idolatry, whatever their modern forms.

2. We have already noted that the results of idolatry and sin are destruction and death. When we look around us we have no difficulty identifying what Paul would see as *results* of the power of sin or idolatry: a person committing suicide, a drug addict, family strife, church divisions, ghettos, social injustices, millions of children dying of hunger and malnutrition, the building of nuclear arsenals, the squandering of natural resources, economic chaos, racism, doctrinal disputes, sexism, rootlessness, selfishness, and so forth. Do we not feel an urgency to address at least one or another of these evils?

We do. So we engage in social action, in church work, in family counseling, in a peace movement, and so forth. We succeed at times, but often we feel powerless. When we think that we have helped to resolve a problem of social injustice, we turn around and discover that it is still there, albeit in another form. How can one begin to address the evils of world hunger and of the nuclear war madness?

Paul would answer: "You cannot correct these evils. The Lord alone can. Proclaim the gospel and have faith."

Of course, Paul's answer leaves us uneasy. We doubt that preaching the gospel is sufficient. Are we not also called to serve our neighbors, to be actively engaged in fighting one or another of these manifestations of evil? I have had such doubts. I recall, for instance, my jealous admiration for the work accomplished by a friend actively engaged in providing medical care for the poor and the deprived. Yet he helped me rediscover the meaning of my own work when, after describing his remarkable service in a slum, he asked me half-jokingly: "And you, what are you doing? After all, what's the use of preparing people for ministry? We need more doctors, more nurses, more social workers in slums, and not more preachers!" After his description of the pitiful situations he encountered daily, I remained speechless. But his question kept nagging me until I discovered that if I had kept Paul's teaching in mind I could have answered him: "How can you call yourself a doctor! You treat the symptoms and leave unattended the disease!"

This perspective contains an essential dimension of Paul's teaching. Whatever the manifestations of evil around us, they are just that, *"manifestations"* of evil. Treating symptoms (the manifestations) is helpful and often necessary. If a person has jumped into a river in an attempt to commit suicide, we need first to pull him or her out of the water if we want to have a chance to help that person in a more fundamental and durable way. But it is useless merely to exhort that person by saying: "Don't jump into the river. You will kill yourself." It is that which pushes this person to commit suicide which must be eradicated. Paul would identify this self-destructive drive as a "power" which keeps that person in bondage. He would call it the power of sin. Such a power can take many forms. It can be the Law as "idol" of the Jews, the "elemental spirits of the universe," the "rulers of this world," that is, natural powers, as well as religious, economic, social, political, and cultural powers. Behind each manifestation of evil there is such a power at work. As long as the power is not defeated, it is bound to continue producing evil manifestations.

3. Contemporary works in the social sciences[13] and in social ethics acknowledge the role of these powers, and are not far from Paul's teaching. The difference is that Paul invites us to look at these powers *from the point of view of the Christ event and of his work of reconciliation.* When evil powers and their manifestations are viewed from this perspective, their true nature, according to the Christian faith, appears.

a. *Any manifestation of evil in our world is perceived to be the result of an idolatry which keeps people in bondage.*

First, recall that, for Paul, an idolatry is the undue absolutization

13. See Peter Berger, *The Sacred Canopy: Elements of a Sociological Theory of Religion* (New York: Doubleday & Co., 1969).

of something good, for instance, a gift from God, or a revelation from God. No wonder idolatry is so fascinating, mesmerizing, and thus powerful. So we cannot reject completely even the worst evil powers. In fact, such a blind rejection of evil powers is powerless because it denies what idolaters rightfully perceive as good. Furthermore, in the process we would be rejecting a good gift from God.

Second, we should recognize that, even though idols are human-made and therefore have "no real existence," they nonetheless have a real power over idolaters and weak believers (1 Cor. 8:1 – 13) which drives them to destroy themselves, human relationships, and the world. Pretending that these idolatrous powers do not exist, because idols have no real existence, is in fact to submit to the powers and play their game.

Take for example the nuclear arms race. Clearly it is a manifestation of evil which leads to the destruction of the human race. It is certainly right to try to slow down the nuclear arms race by applying pressure upon our governments, lobbying for the passage of bills calling for a nuclear freeze, and so forth. But these well-intentioned efforts are largely powerless. Yes, we score "victories." A nuclear freeze resolution is passed by the United States Congress. But the same Representatives and Senators vote shortly thereafter to appropriate the necessary funds to build a new missile system. The problem is that we have not addressed the real issue, namely, what it is that drives us to engage in a nuclear arms race, that is, what is the idolatry which drives us to self-destruction. It is something which we cannot get hold of because it is so pervasive. We are so mesmerized by the manifestation of evil (the nuclear arms race in this example), that we do not notice its direct relation to technology and the fact that we cannot imagine a life without technology. This suggests that technology is one of our idolatries. We can therefore look at it in terms of what Paul says concerning the role of the Law (Torah) for the Jews.

Technology promises life to us (Rom. 7:10). Indeed, technology is good (Rom. 7:12) and brings about many good things: hospitals, medicine, progress in agriculture, world-wide communication, and so forth. But there is something wrong when we cannot imagine a meaningful life apart from technology. We feel that we must protect at all costs—it is "our life"—the technological society we have built and whatever is needed for maintaining that technological society as it is. So, for example, we need to protect the sources of energy, and, of course, the only means of "salvation" from any threat or any problem are technological areas. Technology will save us by developing alternate sources of energy—this is good, in a sense—and by developing more sophisticated weapons to protect this technological society without which no meaningful life is possible.

I am suggesting that as long as we view a certain style of life, a technological life, as the only possible way of life, as an absolute, there is no way out of the nuclear arms race. The problem is not that technology is evil in and of itself. Technology is a good gift from God who gave us the ability to transform our world so as not to be under its power. But we have made out of technology and out of a technological way of life an absolute which now has power over us. This is idolatry. The technological idolatry seems to be a prevalent idolatry of the industrialized world under which are subsumed many kinds of specific idolatries, as the cosmological idolatry of the Hellenistic world in Paul's time took many different specific forms.

b. *We feel totally powerless toward our idolatry. We are under its power and we believe that it will give us the good life, even though we recognize it leads us to death. Even if we are believers, we cannot do anything but submit to its power just as Christ "emptied himself and took the form of a slave" to evil powers (Phil. 2:7).*

In Paul's perspective, knowing, for instance, that the nuclear arms race leads to destruction and making others aware of this fact will not free us from the power of our idol and, consequently, will not prevent us from pursuing death and destruction. As Paul points out, "Though they know God's decree that those who do such things deserve to die, they not only do them but approve those who practice them" (Rom. 1:32). Such is the power of idolatry. It imprisons us in the "mad" logic of our senseless and darkened minds (Rom. 1:21) making us believe that it will give us the good life, even though we can see that it leads us to death.

Believers should not pretend to escape from that hopeless situation, or even try to escape. Just as Abraham had to face the hopeless situation of his death-like body and of the death-like womb of Sarah despite his faith in the promise of an heir, and just as Christ had to face the hopeless situation of the cross, so we also have to face the hopeless character of the situation in which we live. But "in hope [we can believe] against hope" (Rom. 4:18).

   c. *Because of the promise contained in reconciliation, we can trust that God will intervene, or more exactly, that the Lord is in the process of intervening and destroying the power of our idol, through Christ-like manifestations.*

The power of the resurrection—resurrection-like manifestations of God which free us—is at work in our hopeless situation. Yet *if* these resurrection-like manifestations are not recognized for what they are, *if* they are not shown to be the fulfillment of the promise contained in the resurrection of Christ, who is now the Lord putting all his enemies under his feet (1 Cor. 15:24 – 28), *if* the promise itself is not proclaimed (without the promise, how could its fulfillment be recognized, Rom. 10:14), *then* "how could people call upon the name of the Lord" and "be saved" (Rom. 10:13 – 14)?

The urgency to proclaim that the power of God is freeing us from our idolatry, from a specific power of sin, is now clear. How long do we have before a nuclear holocaust? According to Paul, what will free people from the power of their idolatry is not a proclamation of doom showing that idolatry leads them to death. They know it already. Alone the proclamation of the gospel can free people from their idolatry. But it must be a proclamation that the power of God is at work in the hopeless situation of our hearers through cross-like people—people who are themselves powerless under the bondage of the idol—yet, people in whom God intervenes in a resurrection-like fashion.

4. The question is, of course, do we share Paul's faith? Does the church share Paul's faith? I suspect that Paul would see us as "weak believers," that is, as believers still under the power of our "idolatries" (1 Cor. 8:1 – 13) despite our faith. We already know the gospel, that is, the promise. We see the fulfillment of the promise in our individual lives, and are thereby liberated from some of our bondages. But we are too much concerned to hold on to what we believe. Our attitude has a twofold negative effect. On the one hand, we cannot truly love other Christians who have slightly different beliefs than ours. Instead of loving them, we insist on our own way, and refuse to believe all things (1 Cor. 13:4 – 7) because we fail to recognize them as "better than ourselves," that is, as people in whom God manifests himself to us. On the other hand, we are unable to carry out our vocation in the world—proclaiming the gospel as the power of God for salvation—because we fail to recognize God's manifestations in the world.

Our first task as preachers is to help all believers grow in faith by discovering and pointing out how God is at work in the church. In so doing, together we will be strengthened in our faith and be freed from the powers that still enslave us. Our church experience will prepare us to carry out our vocation in the world. We can even say that in itself church experience will already bear witness to, be a demonstration of, the power of God in our society because the powers that still enslave us and from which we will be freed are essentially the same as those which enslave the world. The church's freedom will thus be a type or prefiguration of the world's freedom.

THESIS 14

Our primary task as preachers of Paul's gospel is to call the church and ourselves to faithfulness. Preaching needs to be both a proclamation of the kerygma and of Paul's teaching (the promise) and a proclamation of the fulfillment of the promise in the church. In short, it needs to be a *preaching of the church to the church*.

Notes

1. It is not necessary to insist that Paul systematically proclaimed the church to the church. By constantly referring to God's manifestations in his readers' experience, Paul makes it clear—and does so at crucial points in his arguments.[14] Furthermore, Paul often offers one congregation as an example (or as a type) to other congregations, and vice-versa; for instance, implicitly in 1 Thess. 1:7 – 8, and explicitly in 2 Corinthians 8 (the Macedonians are offered as an example to the Corinthians), and in 2 Corinthians 9 (the Corinthi-

14. Cf. Patte, *PFPG*, 127 – 45.

ans are offered as an example to the Macedonians). Following the model of Paul's letters, our preaching should offer members of the church, or groups within the church, as an example (a type) to each other.

But, should we imitate Paul when, as he does quite frequently, he offers himself as an example (type) to his readers? We now understand that Paul is not arrogant since he "shows off" his own weaknesses—being crucified with Christ—his powerlessness, and how God manifested his power in this powerlessness. This is the way in which Paul offered himself as an example to the Corinthians in 2 Corinthians 12, in a context in which he has to speak, quite exceptionally, of God's manifestations in his own private experience. Paul makes the same case, although indirectly, throughout his letters by the way in which he speaks of himself. He remains quite discreet when describing his private experience—for instance, he says very little about his encounter with the resurrected Christ (1 Cor. 15:8; Gal. 1:16)—and he constantly emphasizes his relationship with others as in the opening and closing of each letter. Still we feel reluctant, and rightly so, to imitate him by offering ourselves as an example to our hearers. Such a proclamation could quickly turn into arrogance. Yet, in one respect, we can follow the example of Paul without risk: we can acknowledge our powerlessness, our lack of knowledge, our weakness in faith. We need to present ourselves as we are, that is, as people who constantly need to grow in the faith by discovering God at work in others, and thus, as people who need to receive faith from others. As preachers we particularly need to be freed from the temptation to see ourselves as better than others because of the "knowledge" we suppose we have. Certainly, we have knowledge to impart, but as Paul would say, it is only the knowledge of the cross (1 Cor. 2:2): a knowledge of our powerlessness and of our lack of any absolute knowledge; a knowledge of the fact that we are constantly in need of "receiving," in need of the grace through which God intervenes and manifests himself to us through Christ-like others. It is as such a person that we can present ourselves as a "type" for our congregations.

2. These last observations imply that our preaching needs to have a very specific form. Involuntarily, through many of our sermons, we convey that we *have* a knowledge which is *the* true knowl-

edge that our hearers need to appropriate, and thereby that we are better than others. This is the case for any sermon which fails to be grounded in a fulfillment of the promise of the gospel in other people. In order to convey the message of the cross, our sermons need to ground their call to faithfulness and their exhortations in the revelations of God *that we have received from others.* In other words, our sermons need to identify people in the church who are bearers of revelation for us, who are Christ-like—cross-like and resurrection-like—for us. In this way our preaching will no longer be grounded in *our* own knowledge or in *our* God-given gifts, but in *what we receive from others in the Church.* In that way our sermons will be what they should be according to Paul. Paraphrasing 1 Cor. 2:2 – 5 and 1 Thess. 1:5, we can say that our sermons will be the demonstration of our powerlessness and of our lack of knowledge; that they will simultaneously demonstrate our faith—how could we perceive these revelations and manifestations of God in our fellow church members without faith?—with "full conviction" about the promise of the gospel, and that they will also be a "demonstration of power" since they will show that the power of God is at work in the church.

3. In our congregations and in the church at large, who are these bearers of revelation and these Christ-like people? How should we identify them? In what situations should we look for them?

The answer to these questions is at first quite surprising, and yet it is clearly the only possible answer from Paul's perspective: *in everybody and in every situation in the church.*[15] Of course, not everything going on in the church is from God! Through faith—that is, by looking around us through the use of the type/promise of the gospel in which we believe—we need to discern how and where God intervenes in our experience through other persons, so much so that we are able to consider them as better than ourselves.

In order to understand why we can discover God's manifestations

---

15. I have suggested above that "our sermons need to identify people in the church who are bearers of revelation for us." We are uneasy, being aware of the danger involved, if certain members of the church are singled out. Others will be jealous, and so forth. But one ought not single out a few individuals. Everybody in the church is bearer of revelation for us although not in the same way. Of course, we cannot refer to "everybody" at once. We need only to refer to a few examples in each sermon, while making clear that we will refer to others at other times. And don't let us forget to do so!

in everybody and in every situation we need to keep in mind the different kinds of divine manifestations that Paul discovered, thanks to the gospel.

a. Paul discovered God's manifestation in "good things" which happened to his churches and himself: the gifts of the Spirit, a safe journey, visiting with the churches, the joy and comfort resulting from the love of a brother (Philemon 4 – 7), the work of faith and labor of love of a church (1 Thess. 1:3), and so forth. Yet we should remember—the Corinthians forgot and went astray—that these "good things" are correctly perceived as manifestations of God, as blessings, when, and only when, they are viewed as resurrection-like, that is, when they are blessings related in one way or another to cross-like situations.

We have no difficulty identifying as manifestations of God the many blessings and good things which take place in the lives of the communities of faith. And we do well when we proclaim them and give thanks for them. But as long as we are sinners—until the Parousia!—all that we perceive as good is not necessarily a gift from God. At times, as sinners, we are bound to identify as "blessing from God" what is "good according to our idol," that is, what satisfies our desires, including the nobler desires. Thus we must "test" everything.

What is truly good—blessing from God—is necessarily related to a cross-like situation. But we need to remember that there are three kinds of relations between blessings and cross-like situations. First, there is *the good which is in bondage* or under the power of evil: Christ, the Son of God, becoming slave of evil powers and being crucified; the Law as revelation from God veiled by the Jews and for the Jews; the creation as work of God in bondage because of idolatries. Second, there is *the good as liberation from bondage:* the resurrection as deliverance from the cross and from death; the Christ-like deliverances from the power of sin, or from the bondage to an idolatry. Third, there is *the good which results from "offering oneself as living sacrifice":* the "work of faith and labor of love" (1 Thess. 1:3) as a gift or fruit of the Spirit.

Before proclaiming the blessings from God we therefore need to test them by making sure that they fit one or the other of the above categories. For this purpose, we first need to identify the cross-like situations in their various forms.

b. For Paul, divine revelations can be found in the worst of sinners since, by definition, sinners are idolaters. In other words, they have made an idol out of something good, a gift of God, a revelation from God.

As we consider the attitude we should have toward "sinners," I deliberately dismiss the view that there is no real difference between "us as sinners" and "them as sinners," a view which we wrongly derive from our confession that "all [we included] are sinners" (Rom. 3:9). Rather, it is precisely because we are sinners, under the power of sin, that we distinguish ourselves from these others who are worse sinners than we are, or that, more candidly, we distinguish ourselves as righteous from the true sinners. We might not recognize that we have this attitude because, in our culture, we often do not think that the term "sinner" applies to such circumstances. Yet we have to acknowledge that in practice we constantly make a distinction between "we the good people" and "they, the evil people, the sinners." Who are they? They are all the people who, in our view, do wrong things or do not do the good things that they should do—according to us. They are also all the church members with whom we disagree about the way of leading a Christian life, about matters concerning church organization and vocation, or even about theological matters. All these people are, in our eyes, wrong, foolish, blasphemous, and thus "sinners," even though we might not use this term. Furthermore it should be emphasized that, despite our limitations, our judgment is often quite valid. Murderers are indeed sinners! Certain ways in which the Christian message is interpreted and put into practice are a mockery of the gospel and are sinful. As we strive to be faithful, we are not like these sinners! This does not mean that we are ourselves sinless. But we need to be realistic about the way in which we view others. As we apply Paul's teaching our inclination to self-righteousness will be taken care of! All that I am trying to say is that in practice we readily identify sinners, and that our identification is not necessarily wrong, although it may be wrong precisely when we are sure it is right!

Let us assume that we are right in our judgment, since, at any rate, this is what we spontaneously believe. What should be our attitude toward those we identify as sinners? Now, for Paul, divine revelations can be found in sinners, that is, in the people whose conduct we disapprove and whose views we reject as wrong and dangerous. Consequently, instead of looking at these "sinners" as people who simply need to be judged, condemned, and corrected, that is, brought back to the right track, we have to look at them as bearers of revelation. Since these people are "sinners," such revelation is hidden, veiled, distorted, enslaved, but it is nonetheless a revelation that we need to receive from these others who, as sinners, are part of our experience. Revelation is offered to us by God through these sinners.

In fact, we cannot hope to carry out faithfully our vocation as long as we do not appropriate such revelation. Of course, it is necessary to distinguish, in the sinners' experience, the manifestation of the wrath of God—that is, the destructive drives and attitudes— from the true revelation which fuels these drives and attitudes after being absolutized. Yet it is clear that this identification of the true revelation demands from us a quite different attitude toward people we consider sinners. Instead of viewing ourselves as *having* something to give to these sinners—the light, the truth, salvation—we need to approach them as people *from whom we need to receive something*. Before saying anything to them, we need to listen, to be silent and to contemplate them as their lives in light of the gospel. In this way we will discover this revelation, this gift from God, this good thing that they have perceived and grasped, although, unfortunately, they have made an idol out of it by holding on to it as if this manifestation of God were the only revelation, the complete and final means of having life. After having received this revelation from them—or having been reminded of it as something which we need to continue acknowledging as a valuable gift from God—we will be in a position to join them, by becoming Greeks with the Greeks (1 Cor. 9:21), by sharing their world, although without conforming to what is sinful in it (Rom. 12:2). Then we may be able to help them, and to be Christ-like for them. But simultaneously, we will have received something from them, something that we need to share with the rest of our fellow believers, always making it clear from whom we have received this insight into God's will and manifestation.

If our preaching proclaims what we have received from others, and uses that as a basis for our call to faithfulness or our exhortations, then our preaching becomes an implicit, or not so implicit, call to consider others, indeed, even sinners, as better than ourselves. They are people from whom we have to receive something essential for our faith, namely revelations from God.

Since, for us, the "sinners" are all the people we disapprove of and with whom we disagree, it is from them all that we have to receive something which is from God, and which should be the basis of our preaching. If, through faith, we consider all these people as better than ourselves, we will not lack subject matter for our sermons!

As a result, several unexpected things will not fail to happen to us first, and then to our congregations. To begin with, we will not be able to hold to what we believe as if it were the complete revelation. What we learn from others becomes just as important as what we already know. We will have adopted an attitude of religious quest. Instead of assuming that we have already reached the goal, we will view ourselves as "running" toward the goal, in quest of it (Phil. 3:12 – 14; 1 Cor. 9:24 – 27). Instead of having a static kind of faith, the routine implementation of the same old truth, in which nothing really happens, we and our congregations will share in Paul's dynamic faith, a race, an adventure which involves the constant discovery of new dimensions of faith. In the process, our preaching will become "a happening," something our congregations can look forward to as always bringing something new to them, indeed a "news," rather than being the constant repetition of a message that they know already, even if we call it the "good news."

c. Something else will not fail to happen to us—even less expected. This will take place when we are confronted with strange cases. Certain people whom we view as wrong, foolish, lacking faith, sinful, are also those through whom something happens that we cannot but view as good. Of course, our first reaction will be to dismiss the good which happens through or in these people as a manifestation of hypocritical attitude, or as meaningless. How can good come out of evil? Yet, when we view these people in the perspective of the gospel we will be led to recognize that in them God is truly at work. We will have to conclude that what we considered to be wrong, foolishness, or lacking in faith, might not be wrong, after all. But then, what is wrong is what led us to see them in a twisted way: our own beliefs which we had taken to be absolute criteria by which to pass judgment on right and wrong. In brief, these people are Christ-like for us. Not only do we have to receive from them a revelation that they had, but also we must receive from them the freedom from bondage to our beliefs. As the Jews were in bondage to the Law, the Word of God that they had transformed into an idol (Romans 7), and as the Corinthians were in bondage to the gospel that they had also transformed into an idol (2 Corinthians 11—13), so we often absolutize our belief system, transforming it into an idol. But now as the Jews (Rom. 8:1 – 7) and Corinthians (2 Cor. 7:8 – 12) were freed from their bondage through Christ, or Christ-like people (Paul and his collaborators), so we need to be freed from our bondage by Christ-like people.

Such an encounter with Christ-like people can be expected more often than we may suppose. This is what is promised in the reconciliation achieved by Christ on the cross. As a result of such discoveries our faith becomes even more dynamic. We are now open to receive from others, and to acknowledge as valid, new insights, new revelations, and new gifts even if they do not conform to the insights, revelations, and gifts we already have. Then we are no longer arrogant, no longer in need of insisting on our own way, and we can believe all things (1 Cor. 13:4 – 7).

Lewis Wilkins, whom I quoted in my Introduction, provides us with several examples of such Christ-like people. In his list of people who "grew in faith," we find many people who had experiences that we can approve without reservation, "good and valid" experiences. Such is the case, for instance, of those who experience growth in faith when they move "from being single to being married," "from being children to being parents." In brief, we do not have any difficulty understanding that such people who received blessings from God—marriage, a child—would grow in faith, a gift from God. The claim that God's gift is received as a result of something which happened beyond the church domain—worship services, Sunday school—seems spurious, since the church acknowledges, in religious ceremonies, marriages and children as blessings from God.

Wilkins also presents the case of the people growing in faith following the death of a parent or of a spouse. Since there are church funeral services and pastoral counseling, we could claim that these people's growth in faith is a blessing directly related to the church. Yet death seems to be a different case. Would we dare to call such an experience a blessing from God? Rather, the death of a loved one is a cross-like experience. Why did these people grow in faith when confronted by such an experience?

Other cases help us address the question, namely the cases of those who are "uprooted" from one place to another, and of those who are fired from a job. Their growth in faith, a gift from God, happens through cross-like events in the secular world. As we well know, these painful experiences are often also liberating experiences. Uprooted from a place or from a job, one is taken away from the life one had, a life that one considered to be a blessing, and often, to be the only possible, and imaginable, kind of life. Such a disruption is a painful experience, but at the same time a liberating experience. One may be forced to look for another kind of life and may discover in the process that, after all, there are other possible kinds of life. Growth in faith can be the consequence of "disruptive" liberation.

Such is the way in which one can interpret one's situation in the perspective of the cross and resurrection if one is unemployed or uprooted. But how should we interpret such a situation if we have a job and have not been uprooted? What should be our response to such people?

Take for example the unemployed people who grow in faith. A common response would be that such unemployed people are a reminder that our jobs are blessings from God, and that we should not take them for granted. True enough. Yet such a response implies an interpretation of the loss of the job as a punishment from God— for having taken it for granted, for not having recognized it as a blessing from God. Such a situation is then perceived as a call to acknowledge our jobs as blessings from God, and eventually a call to be faithful stewards of these gifts from God. But this is not what is involved when one considers the unemployed believers from the point of view of reconciliation and of the gospel as promise. From this perspective, we have to acknowledge that what brought about the growth in faith is the loss of the job. Consequently, the evil that we dread, losing our job, is in fact a good. Indeed, we would do anything to keep our jobs. We are totally devoted to our jobs. Losing them would mean losing an essential part of our lives because our jobs give us security and peace.

In the presence of an unemployed person who grows in faith, we are suddenly confronted with a puzzling alternative. We should not make out of our job an absolute, an idol, even if it is indeed a blessing from God. We should "die" to our job, as Paul and the Jewish Christians died to the Law, and as the Greeks died to their Hellenistic religions. Certainly our job gives a sense of security to us and to our families, but exactly as the Law and the Hellenistic idols gave peace and security, false peace and security (1 Thess. 5:3), to the Jews and the Gentiles. Perceiving unemployed believers as Christ-like people leads us to discover that we may have absolutized our jobs. Indeed, we are ready to do anything to keep our jobs. They are a top priority for us. As a result, we do not have time for other things, for family life, for taking care of our co-workers, for church matters, which are lower in our priorities. In addition, we might even consent to do things that are ethically dubious, if not clearly wrong. Our job is a blessing from God indeed, and we should be thankful. But a job should not become an absolute, an idol, that we should preserve at all costs. We should not serve our job. Work is a gift from God so that we can serve God. Discovering Christ in the unemployed believer who is growing in faith, is being delivered from the bondage to our job—dying to our job (Gal. 2:19) that was supposed to give us life (Rom. 7:10)—so that we can live for Christ.

Wilkins needs to be heard again: some people grow in faith as a result of the experience of moving "from being married to being single." On the basis of scriptural teaching we often view divorce as an evil, as sinful. But such a predicament should be treated exactly as the preceding ones. A divorced believer who grows in faith because of his or her divorce may be a Christ-like person for us. What is called into question is our attitude toward these blessings from God—our marriage and our family. We also are called to die to our marriage and to our family. This does not mean, of course, that we ourselves should seek a divorce, just as dying to the Law did not require the Jewish Christians to abandon their Jewish way of life and to reject the Law (Torah), the Word of God. It means that we should no longer view our marriage or our family as an absolute, as something that we have to preserve at all cost. They are blessings to help us serve God, and not something we should serve. Divorced believers growing in faith are thus Christ-like for us; they free us from our bondage to the idol we might have made out of our marriage or our family. Similarly, those who grow in faith following the death of their spouse, are Christ-like for us, and for the same reasons.

Finally, those who grow in faith as a result of the experience of moving out of the church, a case that Wilkins also discusses, may be Christ-like for us. Such people may free us from bondage to the church as idol, the church which we have absolutized so much that there is no salvation outside of it. Once again, the church is a precious gift from God, but we are easily so devoted to the work of the church, to the activities of the church, that we are not free to recognize God's activity beyond the church. Indeed, the church—its worship services, its Sunday school, its fellowship—is a precious gift from God, yet it should not be viewed as an absolute that we should serve, but rather as a means to help us serve God in the world where God is also at work.

These are only a few examples which are in fact too general to be preached. What is essential? To discover for ourselves and to proclaim to our congregations the Christ-like manifestations that, from the perspective of the gospel, we see in our congregations. *The power of the gospel is manifested for us NOT when we learn a general principle, but when we are confronted by Christ-like manifestations of God in our midst.*

4. If our preaching consists of a constant proclamation of such a fulfillment of the gospel in other people in, or related to, our congregations, it will be an invitation to our congregations to embrace the same faith. Such preaching will foster a loving interaction between the church members, although the church life will not be

free from tensions. On the one hand, each member will be looking
at others to discover what he or she needs to receive from them—a
gift, a revelation, an insight that the others have. On the other
hand, because members in a church are different from each other,
they will often see in each other Christ-like people who challenge
them to consider as a loss that in which they have put absolute confi-
dence (Phil. 3:4 – 7). In either case, they will truly love each other.
Each will consider the other as better than himself or herself, learn
from the other, and grow in faith thanks to the other.

This love is another manifestation of God among us, another
blessing from God that we can proclaim and need to proclaim. Such
a church will also be a "thanksgiving church," a church which will
celebrate all these gifts of God that have been identified and
received from others.

Yet such preaching will also be a call to faithfulness in another
sense. It will be a call to fulfill our vocation and to offer ourselves as
a living sacrifice, and therefore a call to perform what Paul called
"work of faith and labor of love." (1 Thess. 1:3)

Fulfillment of our vocation demands that we recognize, through
faith, the gifts, insights, and revelations that sinners have, despite
the fact that they have distorted these gifts by absolutizing them and
transforming them into idols. In the process, the manifestation of
the "wrath of God" upon these people is also revealed to us (Rom.
1:18). That is, we can recognize their self-destructive attitudes and
the powers which keep them in bondage. Yet we know that this
manifestation of the wrath of God is not a permanent punishment
that God wants to inflict upon them. The will of God is that they be
freed from their self-destructive attitudes, and our ministry, and
indeed that of any believer, is a ministry of reconciliation (2 Cor.
5:18).

We begin fulfilling our vocation toward these sinners as soon as
we recognize the gifts from God that they have received and that we
affirm. By so doing, we have already become Jews with the Jews,
Greeks with the Greeks, weak with the weak (1 Cor. 9:19 – 23). We
have entered their world, consenting to share with them the precious gift of God that they have. Yet, we cannot view their gift as an
absolute and live exclusively for it as they do. This is so because we

also are receiving from other members of the church other gifts from God, and we are constantly looking for other gifts from God in still other people. Consequently, the gifts of God which sinners have cannot become absolute for us since they must be set side by side with other gifts that we receive through other members of the church.

In other words, by the mere fact that we are viewing all others in the church as better than ourselves, we cannot get involved with sinners in their "idolatry." We enter their world, share with them the gift they have received from God, but refuse to absolutize this gift.

For example, consider a person who has made an absolute out of a particular form of service, and is thereby a "sinner." We can recognize that such a service—which might be a very altruistic service— has been absolutized, when it has become destructive, as any idol is. It demands that the value of other people's service be denied, and thus that other people's needs be neglected. As such it denies the love relationship with other members of the church and thus destroys the community. Furthermore, for the person involved, it becomes self-destructive, a self-destructive passion. Our response to such a situation needs to be twofold. On the one hand, we need to affirm the value of their service, and the talent to carry it out, as a blessing from God and as an important way to serve God. Thus we will be involved in supporting and helping that person to serve. On the other hand, we simultaneously need to refuse to be associated with any of its destructive dimensions. We must deny the absolute importance of their service. Now, for the person who is so passionately committed to this service, we are hypocrites, affirming the value of something and not carrying it through, or even undermining it. Indeed, we will then be rejected, criticized. Things will become worse as we alternatively continue to affirm the value of the service and the talent of that person, and yet show by our attitude that, at certain points, we refuse to get involved, or directly express our disagreement.

The result of this attitude is not glorious! We have only managed to create tensions, mistrust, and rejection. This is what happens when we offer ourselves as living sacrifice (Rom. 12:1). It brings about a cross-like situation. But we can do so with trust and hope that God will intervene in a resurrection-like manifestation so as to make us fully Christ-like for this person. All we can do is remain faithful in our ambivalent attitude toward the person, toward her or his service and talent. The situation can only be resolved through a manifestation of God. Our work of faith and labor of love can be successful only if they involve a direct manifestation of God. As a result of such a manifestation of God, the attitude toward the service to which he or she is devoted would change, and thus this person would be liberated from bondage to his or her service while continuing to perform it.

Through our preaching, therefore, we can and must proclaim Christ-like manifestations that result from the fact that faithful people fulfill their vocation toward others. We need to give thanks for these works of faith and love. But, as is also clear, such a preaching and the faith that it communicates will not effect a church life without tension. In fact, as long as we are sinners, that is, as long as we are a community of human beings, living together prior to the Parousia, our love for each other will necessarily engender tensions and crises. Because of our love and faith, we will want to become Christ-like for each other, and thus risk cross-like situations with trust and hope that God will intervene in a resurrection-like fashion.

Tensions also existed in Paul's churches. We wish for a smoother style of church life, thinking that, somehow, the problems that Paul had to face have, by now, been overcome. But, in fact, the problem is sin, and it remains our problem! Furthermore, it is important to note that Paul did not try to minimize tensions. On the contrary, as can be seen in his letters, Paul often provoked trouble and created tension by his attitudes and actions. Paul was merely fulfilling his vocation, being Christ-like for other people, exasperating them by affirming the gifts of God that they had received and simultaneously refusing to consider these gifts as absolutes, for the sake of other people in whom he also saw God at work.

It is this church, with all its tensions resulting from its attempts to be faithful and loving, which is called to witness to the world, to *proclaim the world to the world,* just as our preaching is a proclamation of the church to the church.

THESIS 15

It is such a church, with all its imperfections, its tensions, its crises resulting from its love and faith, which is to be the body of Christ for the world, not only by proclaiming the gifts of God that the world has received, but also by dying to the world through its refusal to absolutize any of these gifts. As such the church can expect to be "crucified," rejected, scorned, but the church can also trust and hope that God will intervene in a resurrection-like fashion.

Notes

1. Most of what we said in Thesis 14 concerning the discovery of manifestations of God in the church, the proclamation of these manifestations, and the interaction among believers in the church, could be repeated here about the relations between the church and the world by simply changing some of the terms. For Paul, there are no clear boundaries between the church and the world. As Wayne Meeks says, following his examination of this relationship from several perspectives, "This ambiguity about the community's boundaries was one of the important bequests by the Pauline Christians to the literary canon of the later church."[16] He attributes the openness toward the world to the missionary zeal of the Pauline communities "which saw in the outsider a potential insider and did not want to cut off communication with him or her."[17] Meeks notes the same ambiguity in his study of "rituals" which enhance the coherence of the Christian group, and thus potentially establish boundaries between the Church and the outsiders, and yet, in 1 Corinthians 8—10, rituals are discussed in a context presenting the complex interaction of believers and the world.[18] He sees this attitude as an anomaly. "A sect that claims to be the unique possessor of what it

16. Meeks, *The First Urban Christians*, 169.
17. Ibid., 107.
18. Ibid., 140 – 63.

construes to be a universally desirable value—a monopoly on salvation—does not necessarily welcome free interchange with outsiders; more often the contrary."[19] Meeks's perplexity, as indicated by
his frequent use of terms like "ambiguous,"[20] would have been allevi-
ated if he had recognized that the Christian communities faithful to
Paul's teaching did not conceive of themselves in this way. As we
noted in our discussion of Thesis 14, for Paul, the church is not the
"possessor" of the Truth, and cannot be construed as having a
"monopoly on salvation." God has the monopoly on salvation! The
church is an eschatological community which, through love and
faith, discovers IN OTHERS God's power of salvation at work.
Manifestations of God, gifts of the Spirit, revelations are, for the
church, a new fulfillment of the gospel of Christ, as promise and
type, and preliminary manifestations of that which will be fully
established at the Parousia. Believers, far from possessing a Truth,
always need to discover and to receive revelations that they do not
have, and to join God in his action. Where will they discover these
new manifestations of God or of Christ? In each other, of course.
But also in outsiders, in the world. This is what is promised by the
cross as the reconciliation of the *world* to God (2 Cor. 5:19), and
what is hoped for at the Parousia, when all the "powers" will at last
be defeated, and when the Law (Torah) will be fully unveiled liberating the Jews from their bondage (Rom. 11:11 – 26) and when the
creation itself will be freed from its own enslavement (Rom.
8:18 – 25).

Consequently, believers can expect to discover in the world, as
they do in the church, not only true revelations, true "good," distorted by bondage to idolatries, but also Christ-like manifestations
of God. Thus, the attitude of believers toward outsiders should be
the same as their attitude toward each other in the church. This is
one of the main points of 1 Cor. 8:1—11:1. Toward "outsiders" one

19. Ibid., 107.

20. Meeks' expression of his perplexity is to be positively acknowledged. This perplexity is the recognition that his sociological analysis reveals an unexpected picture
of the relationship between the Pauline communities and outsiders. This is what his
approach reveals and Meeks is to be credited for not trespassing the boundaries of
what his methodology can establish. It is a study of Paul's system of convictions (using
a structural exegetical method) which allows one to elucidate the Pauline conviction
about the nature of the Christian church and its vocation.

needs to be "Jew with the Jews" or "Greek with the Greeks." Toward
"insiders" one needs to be "weak with the weak." We have noted
that such an attitude is based upon love and faith, gifts which lead
the believers to "consider others as better than themselves."

What distinguishes the church from the world is that the church
is a community of believers, a *koinonia*, that is, a community of
people freed from idolatry and constantly in the process of being
freed from it by the very fact that they "believe all things" because
they recognize that they are always in need of receiving new views
and new gifts from others who are different from them. Consequently, they are in a position to discern in the world what is truly
from God from what is idolatrous. What is truly from God is
defined as that which they can receive from the world without
denying what they receive from other believers. As one becomes
Greek with the Greeks or Jew with the Jews, that which would be
offensive to other members of the church and risk making them fall
cannot be from God. But, vice-versa, what would be offensive to
the Greeks or to the Jews, that is, what would prevent their being
freed from their idolatrous bondages and having faith, cannot be
from God, even if it is in the church (1 Cor. 10:23 – 32). In other
words, whatever in the church denies the possibility of discovering
in the world and receiving from the world revelations from God,
and thus whatever in the church prevents the believers from becoming "world with world," has to be idolatrous. Such is the case when
the Church claims to be the "unique possessor of . . . a universally
desirable value," and to have "a monopoly on salvation."[21] This is
what Paul expresses in 1 Cor. 10:32—11:1:

> Give no offense to Jews or to Greeks or to the church of God, just as
> I try to please all men in everything I do, not seeking my own advan-
> tage, but that of many, that they may be saved. Be imitators of me, as
> I am of Christ.

2. What then should be our attitude toward the world in the
present situation? How should we witness to the gospel as the power
of God for salvation in the world? Exactly as we witness to it in the
church. There is no point in repeating what I have already said. The

21. Meeks, *The First Urban Christians*, 107.

suggestions I made in Thesis 14, Note 3 can be easily applied to our relation to the world.

A concrete example could be helpful, but, in fact, I have already proposed one by briefly discussing the attitude that the church should have vis-a-vis the technological society in which we live (see Thesis 13, Note 3). Granted, it is a quite superficial example. An extended discussion would merely rehearse much of what has been said by Gabriel Vahanian, a theologian who strives to be faithful to Paul's teaching.[22] Three concluding notes will therefore suffice.

a. In contemporary Western culture, a post-Christian culture, the primary mission of the church toward the world should not be just the proclamation of the *kerygma*. At the very least, the broad features of the *kerygma*, Christ's death and resurrection, are widely known, even though they are often explicitly or implicitly considered foolish. Consequently, the transmission of the Christian faith is not so much a matter of proclamation "in word," as it is primarily a matter of demonstration of "power" and of "full conviction" (1 Thess. 1:5). This is to say that the church needs to make itself "Christ-like" for the world. The task entails, as is clear by now, entering the idolatrous realms of the world, affirming the true "good" or revelation which is therein, refusing to conform to these idolatries, being rejected and/or being persecuted, and demonstrating one's "full conviction" by trusting that the Lord will intervene "in power." The church also needs to identify Christ-like manifestations that it discovers in the secular world itself. In brief, the church needs to proclaim, on the one hand, the good, the revelation, which is veiled in the idolatries of the world, and, on the other hand, disclose the Christ-like manifestations in the secular world. It needs to proclaim the world to the world, that is, to reveal to the world the Lord's gifts and manifestations of which it is already the beneficiary.

b. In order to carry out such a vocation, the church needs to be a "contemplating" and "thanksgiving" community. Looking at the world through faith, that is, from the perspective of the promise of

22. Gabriel Vahanian, *God and Utopia: The Church in a Technological Civilization* (New York: Seabury Press, 1977).

the gospel, the church can identify the gifts of God that the world has transformed into idols, and also the fulfillment of the promise of the reconciliation which is already to be found in the world.

Yet the task is not easy. The church and its members belong to the world, and, more often than not, are also in bondage to idolatries of the world. Consequently, there is no way that, as individuals, we will be able to discern what is truly going on in the world. We would right away be mesmerized, or would remain mesmerized, by the power of the world's idolatries. Only as a community of believers can we identify the world's idolatries and become Christ-like, "offer ourselves as living sacrifice" (Rom. 12:1) for the world. For indeed, as members of a faithful community we consider each other as better than ourselves. Consequently, we cannot accept any view as an absolute because it would necessarily lead us to reject our brothers and sisters who have different views. In other words, the very pluralism of the church, as a faithful and loving community accepting the inevitable tensions brought about by a diversity of beliefs, enables the church to carry out its vocation in the world without falling prey to its idolatries.

As we, members of the body of Christ, enter the contemporary secular world and contemplate it we can expect to find that the most powerful and prevalent modern "idolatries" are secular in character. In other words, we should not primarily look for those idolatries in the religious realm of modern people's experience, although we can expect that they will, at times, take the garb of traditional religions. Consequently, it is likely that we will have to express the fulfillment of the gospel in secular language. Our proclamation to the world, therefore, will have to relate secular events to the religious events of the *kerygma*, as Paul related the experience of Hellenistic people to the events of a *kerygma* expressed in Jewish concepts.

c. As preachers to the church our role is primarily to call our congregations to a faithful fulfillment of their vocation (see Thesis 14) and to lead them on this path.

Once again, we should not pretend to have all the answers and to know the path. What we noted above (Thesis 14) regarding the impossibility for an individual to discern by himself or herself the fulfillment of the gospel in the world, also applies to preachers! Consequently, our role is to lead our congregations into a community contemplation of the world from the perspective of the gospel. Thus we need to meditate on Paul's letters while we contemplate the world, and to contemplate the world while we meditate on Paul's letters. Of course, we should avail ourselves of the work of those who devote themselves to such a twofold contemplation, namely, to theologians such as Vahanian.

A proclamation to the church of the fulfillment of the gospel in the world is also necessary. Once again, it will be unsettling and often controversial preaching. It will not satisfy either the political conservatives or the religious liberal because it will point out the (idolatrous) bondage which leads the world to destruction. It will also displease both the political or social activist and the religious conservative because it will refuse to condemn the evil world and will affirm "good things" that we have to receive from it.

Such preaching will leave us vulnerable on all sides. Yet, this is what happens to someone who knows nothing except Jesus Christ and him crucified (1 Cor. 2:2). Such preaching does not merely express in words the message of the cross, but truly embodies it in its vulnerability, with the full conviction that the power of God, that is, the power of the cross and of the resurrection, will also be manifested. By our preaching we become Christ-like, or more precisely, cross-like, for our congregations and for the world, with the hope that the gospel as the power of God for salvation will be manifested, and that, as a consequence, our congregations will themselves become Christ-like for others and for us. Then it becomes clear that, as "there is neither Jew nor Greek, there is neither slave nor free, there is neither male nor female" (Gal. 3:28), there is neither preacher nor lay people, but rather one body of Christ, all the members of which have the same vocation—"offering themselves as a living sacrifice" (Rom. 12:1)—which they can carry out only insofar as they are "all one in Christ Jesus" (Gal. 3:28).

4
Preaching Paul
in a Worship Service

The preceding pages should not be taken as a recipe for successful preaching of Paul or for witnessing to the power of the gospel. They are very incomplete "Theses" and "Notes" which, I hope, will invite preachers and lay people alike to go back to Paul's letters. If we want to heed Paul's exhortation to imitate him as he imitates Christ (1 Cor. 11:1), then we need to ponder his letters carefully again and again in order to discover how and where he sees manifestations of the power of the gospel, so that in turn we may identify them in our own experience. Thus we must read Paul's letters in a special way, paying special attention to the manner in which the apostle relates various aspects of his experience and of the church's experience by considering them through faith. The present book merely suggests some broad results of such a reading. The more complete exegesis presented in *Paul's Faith and the Power of the Gospel* provides further guidelines for such a reading, and a more detailed understanding of where Paul sees God at work. Books, though, should not replace the believers' meditation of Paul's letters. It is when we contemplate the specific situations in the church and in the world which confront us that passages of Paul's letters, which seemed to us to be unimportant, suddenly make sense. In these passages we can now recognize a "type" of what is happening in front of us. If indeed Paul's gospel promises that the power of God is at work in our present, then only when we look for the fulfillment of the promise in the concreteness of our lives, can we truly expect to understand the Gospel as the "power of God for salvation" (Rom. 1:16).

By now it should be clear that, from Paul's perspective, such meditation cannot merely be individual and private. Only as a

community of believers—contemplating, and meditating, and giving thanks together—are we in a position to discover the full range
of manifestations of God's power in our present. Preaching Paul is
therefore not merely something which happens during the worship
of a community, but rather is something which must have its roots
in, and be fed by communal worship. Preaching Paul leads to and
demands a special kind of worship which can fit in the context of
many traditional liturgies.

Christian worship needs to be a celebration (1 Cor. 5:8), a service
of thanksgiving. It is easy enough to make sure that the worship
service culminates in such thanksgiving by adapting concluding
prayers (e.g., pastoral prayers, prayers following the celebration of
the Lord's Supper, etc.). Similarly, other elements of the liturgy
need to be oriented toward thanksgiving. Is it not the case, in many
instances, that the call to worship is already a call to celebration? Is
it not possible to present the first part of the worship service as a
preparation to give thanks? How could we really expect to discover
God's manifestations, if we are not reconciled with God and if we
are not assured that God frees us from sin? How could we give
thanks if we do not listen to Scripture and its promises? And thus,
should we not confess our faith in God who gave us the promises and
who is faithful? Furthermore, without Scripture, how could we discover God's fulfillment of the promises in our present? And how
could we give thanks, if we did not know how to discover these fulfillments around us? And how would we know without preaching?
It is not therefore a matter of abandoning traditional liturgy to
which the community is accustomed, but of orienting it toward
thanksgiving. For the Greeks, it will be a Greek thanksgiving service, for the Jews, it will be a Jewish thanksgiving service! The major
difficulty will be to insure that it is a truly communal celebration of
the *present* manifestations of God, a celebration rooted in and fed
by the contemplation and meditation of the community. Certain
traditions may have liturgies flexible enough to accommodate
direct participation of the worshiping community. In many other
cases such participation is not possible. A solution could involve
communal preparation of worship services—for instance, different
groups taking turn to prepare a worship service with the preacher

over a period of several weeks, in order to allow for necessary time of contemplation, meditation, and sharing.

Even though it respects the traditional liturgy, this reorientation of the worship service toward a communal celebration of the present manifestations of God may be, at first, quite threatening to many members of our congregations. After all, the celebration will involve giving thanks for God's manifestations in people who were despised as "sinners" and "ungodly" (Rom. 4:5), who have no recognized religious authority, or simply who are not worthy of attention. Since they manifest the folly of the cross, such worship services cannot but be controversial. Tension is unavoidable, especially because a liturgy also involves acting out this celebration by assigning a visible place in the worship service to the formerly despised people in whom God's manifestation is recognized. For instance, in the case of a congregation which recognizes religious authority exclusively in the clergy, lay people could be given an active role in the worship service, so as to manifest that we, as preachers, do not have a monopoly on God's revelation and indeed need to be led in worship by lay people. In the case of a congregation which acknowledges the religious authority of men alone, women could be asked to lead the liturgy, and women ministers could be invited as guest preachers. A wealthy suburban congregation could manifest its solidarity with poor inner-city congregations by demonstrating in one way or another how much it has to receive from these poor churches, and indeed from the poor.

These examples cannot be in any way regarded as prescriptions, since liturgical acts as well as the rest of the worship service and our preaching need to be a communal celebration of what has been recognized as the present manifestations of God by the contemplation and meditation of the community. In other words, innovations in worship services should not be of such a nature as to prevent members of a community from worshiping. These innovations should have their roots in the community's contemplation, otherwise they are artificial, useless, and even destructive, because they originate in a group which self-confidently sees itself as possessing a truth while forgetting it also needs to receive something from the rest of the community which does not have this truth. One is easily

tempted to make striking iconoclastic gestures, as some of the
Corinthians did by eating meat sacrificed to idols (1 Cor. 8:1—
11:1). As Paul points out, there is nothing wrong with such iconoclastic gestures in and of themselves. But Paul emphasizes that we
must remember the weak believers and avoid being a "stumbling
block" to them (1 Cor. 8:9, 10, 31 – 33). This does not mean that our
worship services and our proclamation should shy away from the
bold affirmation of God's manifestations in those whom weak
believers view as "sinners." But God's manifestations in the weak
believers also need to be respected and celebrated in our worship
services. Those who view themselves as strong believers need to celebrate as Christ-like those whom they despise as the weak, tradition-
alist believers. Then the Christian community will truly be one,
glorifying "with one voice . . . the God and Father of our Lord Jesus
Christ" (Rom. 15:6), as Paul says in conclusion to his exhortations
regarding the weak and the strong believers (Rom. 14:1—15:6).

The entire worship service thereby becomes a celebration of the
manifestations of God's power for salvation in the present of the
church. It is a communal service of thanksgiving through which the
community of believers can perceive its vocation toward the world,
and prepare to offer itself in living sacrifice for the world (Rom.
12:1). Worship is a communal service of thanksgiving in the context
of which preaching will, quite normally, be "not only in word, but
also in power" (1 Thess. 1:5), not only a proclamation of the
kerygma but also of the power of God for salvation.

Fortress Press Resources
for the Study of Saint Paul

Beker, J. C. *Paul's Apocalyptic Gospel: The Coming Triumph of God.* Philadelphia: Fortress Press, 1982.

_____. *Paul the Apostle: The Triumph of God in Life and Thought.* Philadelphia: Fortress Press; Edinburgh: T. & T. Clark, 1980.

Davies, W. D. *Jewish and Pauline Studies.* Philadelphia: Fortress Press; London: SPCK, 1983.

_____. *Paul and Rabbinic Judaism: Some Rabbinic Elements in Pauline Theology.* Fourth edition, with new Preface. Philadelphia: Fortress Press, 1980.

Francis, Fred O., and J. Paul Sampley. *Pauline Parallels.* Revised edition. Philadelphia: Fortress Press, 1984.

Georgi, Dieter. *The Opponents of Paul in Second Corinthians: A Study of Religious Propaganda in Late Antiquity.* First English edition, Enlarged. Philadelphia: Fortress Press; Edinburgh: T. & T. Clark, 1985.

Hock, Ronald F. *The Social Context of Paul's Ministry: Tentmaking and Apostleship.* Philadelphia: Fortress Press, 1980.

Holmberg, Bengt. *Paul and Power: The Structure of Authority in the Primitive Church as Reflected in the Pauline Epistles.* Philadelphia: Fortress Press, 1980.

Jewett, Robert. *A Chronology of Paul's Life.* Philadelphia: Fortress Press; London: SCM Press, 1979.

Käsemann, Ernst. *Perspectives on Paul.* Eng. trans. Margaret Kohl. Philadelphia: Fortress Press, 1971.

Keck, Leander. *Paul and His Letters.* Proclamation Commentaries. Philadelphia: Fortress Press, 1979.

Luedemann, Gerd. *Paul, Apostle to the Gentiles: Studies in Chronology*. Foreword by John Knox. Eng. trans. F. Stanley Jones. Philadelphia: Fortress Press, 1984.

Patte, Daniel. *Paul's Faith and the Power of the Gospel: A Structural Introduction to the Pauline Letters*. Philadelphia: Fortress Press, 1983.

Sampley, J. Paul. *Pauline Partnership in Christ: Christian Community and Commitment in Light of Roman Law*. Philadelphia: Fortress Press, 1980.

Sanders, E. P. *Paul, the Law, and the Jewish People*. Philadelphia: Fortress Press, 1983.

———. *Paul and Palestinian Judaism: A Comparison of Patterns*. Philadelphia: Fortress Press; London: SCM Press, 1977.

Sandmel, Samuel. *The Genius of Paul: A Study in History*. Philadelphia: Fortress Press, 1979.

Scroggs, Robin. *Paul for a New Day*. Philadelphia: Fortress Press, 1977.

Stendahl, Krister. *Paul Among Jews and Gentiles and Other Essays*. Philadelphia: Fortress Press, 1976.

Theissen, Gerd. *The Social Setting of Pauline Christianity: Essays on Corinth*. Edited and translated and with an Introduction by John H. Schütz. Philadelphia: Fortress Press; Edinburgh: T. & T. Clark, 1982.

Commentaries

Betz, Hans Dieter. *Galatians: A Commentary on Paul's Letter to the Churches in Galatia*. Hermeneia—A Critical and Historical Commentary on the Bible. Philadelphia: Fortress Press, 1979.

Conzelmann, Hans. *1 Corinthians: A Commentary on the First Epistle to the Corinthians*. Eng. trans. J. W. Leitch. Hermeneia—A Critical and Historical Commentary on the Bible. Philadelphia: Fortress Press, 1975.

Ebeling, Gerhard. *The Truth of the Gospel: An Exposition of Galatians*. Eng. trans. David E. Green. Philadelphia: Fortress Press, 1985.

Nygren, Anders. *Commentary on Romans*. Eng. trans. Carl C. Rasmussen. Philadelphia: Fortress Press, 1949.

Index of Biblical Passages